BECAUSE I MADE YOU THAT WAY

THE REMARKABLE GIFT OF FOCUS

R.D. KONCERAK

WESTBOW
PRESS®
A DIVISION OF THOMAS NELSON
& ZONDERVAN

WestBow Press books may be ordered through booksellers or by contacting:

WestBow Press
A Division of Thomas Nelson & Zondervan
1663 Liberty Drive
Bloomington, IN 47403
www.westbowpress.com
844-714-3454

Scripture quotations marked KJV are taken from the Holy Bible, King James Version.

Scripture quotations marked NIV are taken from the Holy Bible, New International Version®, NIV®. Copyright © 1973, 1978, 1984 by Biblica, Inc.™ Used by permission of Zondervan. All rights reserved worldwide.

ISBN: 979-8-3850-0375-4 (sc)
ISBN: 979-8-3850-0373-0 (hc)
ISBN: 979-8-3850-0374-7 (e)

Library of Congress Control Number: 2023913793

Print information available on the last page.

WestBow Press rev. date: 11/08/2023

This book is dedicated to Mike Stephens, who baptized my children and ministered to my family,

to John Pearson, who helped make this book better,

and of course, to these intentional friends who made this book possible:
Brian Cummings
Evan Haskins
Rob Lemcke
Alvaro Lima
Caio Lima
Richard Rotondo
Ryan Zernach

An unexamined life is not worth living.
—Socrates

*God is a comedian playing to an audience
that's too afraid to laugh.*
—Voltaire

CONTENTS

Introduction ix

Chapter 1: The Lens 1

Chapter 2 and Group One: How You Were Born 8

  1. You Were Born Without a Value System 12

  2. You Are an Astonishingly Forgetful Creature 27

  3. You Are Drawn to Indulge Your Self-Interest 34

  4. You Live in a Fallen World 39

  Group One Discussion Questions and Further
  Reading 45

Chapter 3 and Group Two: What You Have 47

  5. You Were Born with a Desire to Worship 50

  6. You Were Born with a Rebellious Nature 54

  7. You Were Born with Special Gifts and Abilities ... 62

  8. You Crave Relationships 72

  Group Two Discussion Questions and Further
  Reading 83

Chapter 4 and Group 3: What You Want...........................85

   9. You Want Money, Wealth and Power 85

   10. You Are Driven to Satisfy Your Passions...............94

   11. You Want to Pursue Habits 101

   12. You Want to Lead Yourself.................................. 114

   Group Three Discussion Questions and Further
      Reading 120

Epilogue: Of the Things Which Are In Our Power -
Epictetus 122

Epilogue 2: A World of Magic and Mystery -
Frederick Buechner 125

About the Author... 126

INTRODUCTION

Have you ever wondered why you want certain things? Why you behave in certain ways and react in certain ways? Why you *crave* certain attentions, harbor abominable thoughts, and ponder vast, contemplative questions?

If you asked God, I believe He would tell you, *"It's because I made you that way."*

The mission of this book is to persuade you that your life and personality are evidence of divine design. That your *very nature* attests to the *personality* of God. Rick Warren opened his book, *The Purpose Driven Life*, with the now famous phrase "It's not about you." I believe that is true. But *it is* about knowing *who you are* -- and why your understanding of who you are matters.

This is a journal of contrived explanations from God. It is not an instruction manual, and it's not a manifesto for your life. These contentions offer an explanation for why God made you the way that you are. Not your flesh and bone, but your mind, your will, and your spirit. There aren't many Bible verses referenced in these chapters, and that is for a very good reason. While few would argue that the Bible offers worthwhile principles for living, *the*

Bible is not a reference of authority to someone who hasn't accepted it as truth. We are called to believe the claims of Jesus based on the testimony of people who were actually with Him, but we live in a world of "fake news." So rather than wrestle with ideology, how about we reverse the focus of our lens…and consider *ourselves* as a basis for the existence of a Creator? In pondering *human* ponderings, let us consider our *personal* experience as evidence of a *divine personality!*

We make choices every day that affect the course of our lives. Precarious though it is, we can alter our path with a single (intentional or not) decision. And—like it or not—*other people* make choices that alter our lives, too. This can happen at any moment. In an instant.

It is uncomfortable to acknowledge that you don't have control over many things that happen in your life. But you can—and you *do* decide how you will *respond* to every single one of those happenings. That is something that makes you special. It's your superpower. It is free will.

While our course is inherently unstable, we *pursue* our lives along a path that we *believe* that we choose. We *seek* relevance and enjoyment along our path, and we *hope* for fulfillment along the way. How we perceive our journey matters. And that is why this little book was written.

I wrote this book for men. I believe I am "sufficiently common" that most guys will understand the way I think and present these assembled subjects. While I'm confident that most women would agree with these contentions, I do *not* presume that I know how a woman's mind works. If this book hits its mark, readers of these pages will be surprised at how *intentionally* and *purposefully* God has designed us guys. If I'm *really* successful, men will chuckle as they see themselves reflected in these words. And women will roll their eyes in agreement. *"Yep, that's him all right!"*

The contentions in *Because I Made You That Way* (BIMYTW) are presented in three parts: *How You Were Born*, *What You Have*, and *What You Want*. This isn't a long book. At 30,843 words, it's less than half the length of contemporary volumes. I've done my best to keep each subject short and to the point. In these chapters, you'll find thoughts and ideas that I hope will drive home each contention...with tongue-in-cheek humor along the way. I hope that you find these chapters as entertaining as you find them revealing... because reading isn't enjoyable if you're not drawn to turn the page! Gentle reader, I am confident there is plenty here to capture your attention.

Here are the contentions:

I: *How You Were Born*

1. **You were born without a value system.** You are capable of incredible goodness...and unspeakable evil. The lens you acquire for focus and perspective will shape your personal value system. Without a developed value system, your mind pursues thoughts that are driven by your environment...and perhaps by what you had for dinner last night.

2. **You were born a forgetful creature.** Incredibly so. I can't remember why just now...but keep reading and we'll come back to this later.

3. **You were born with a desire to indulge your self-interest.** You were *not* born with a sacrificial spirit.

   Those are only three of the twelve contentions, and already your stomach has begun to tighten. Am I right?

4. **You were born into a fallen world.** This is *not* the creation that you were designed for. That is why you struggle to fit in.

II: *What You Have*

5. **You have a desire to worship.** You were created with a desire to worship something. And so you do.

6. **You have a rebellious nature.** You do. **Yes,** you do. **I said YES YOU DO!**

7. **You were born with gifts and abilities.** You are equipped in ways that other creatures just aren't. You are capable of amazing things...if given the opportunity and conditions to do them. *If you judge a fish by its ability to climb a tree...*

8. **You have a craving for relationships.** Yeah, all sorts of cravings. We'll get to that.

III: *What You Want*

9. **You *want* money, wealth and power**, but you are *not* designed to handle them well. Now isn't *that* a topic worth exploring?

10. **You are driven to satisfy your passions. If you cannot find admirable means, you will pursue *less* than admirable means to do so.** Most guys understand this. It's a corollary to #3.

11. **You want to pursue habits that are good for you, but there is only so much discipline to go around**. This becomes apparent in the fullness of time. Some guys only get this one when struck with reality. Struck. In the head. With a chair.
12. **You want to lead your*self* well, but you can't.** Truth and objectivity *must* be separate from your condition. We are born to form opinions about our environment. You were not created to be objective. Nobility is *inspired and acquired*, not *born and worn.*

This book is predominantly about sense. Both our *senses* and the practicality of *common* sense. The purpose of our senses is to help us interpret the world around us. Our senses *enable* us to evaluate our world, but they don't entitle us to answers. *Perceptions* are what we gain through the *use* of our senses. Our senses enable us to feel out reality—and consider how reality relates to us. *Common* sense is what helps us make collective *sense* of our senses. And the coordination of these processes is what enables us ultimately to employ free will…and make choices.

This is not a self-help book. Perhaps that is obvious by now. These are assertions that describe *who* you are because of the way that you were made. I contend that God designed you with instincts, drives, and ambitions. He designed you to navigate best by adopting *His* perspectives. Using His *lens*. And God created you to recognize your need for Him.

No one can be forced to accept a Christian lens. As former Attorney General John Ashcroft put it, *Christianity is not an imposition—it's an inspiration!*

Dear reader, should you determine that there is wisdom in this book, know that your author is living proof that wisdom is *not* something we're all born with. People like me have had learning knocked into 'em while living life's adventures...and then fortunately soothed with the salve of divine intervention. Mine has been a worthwhile life so far, I think, as it has brought me to accomplish these pages. And writing about it was cheaper than therapy.

This then, is a testimony. A *testimony* is a statement of things that one knows to be true. This book offers an explanation for why you are wired the way that you are. Experience has shown me that Christianity is not about what happens after you die. It's about how you were created to *live*.

> "When the bible says that God is righteous, it means He is completely just and fair; He never exploits, or abuses. God's work perfectly reflects this same righteousness. **This is hard for modern people, who live in the most authority-averse culture in world history.** Much in the Word seems on the surface unfair and even exploitative to us. However, this is the testimony of millions of people—and of the Word itself; If you will trust God's word, "thoroughly testing" it in the crucible of your own life over the years, you will find it not

*only true, but also delightful. You will come
to love it."*
> \- Timothy Keller, *The Songs of Jesus*,
> November 17 (emphasis added)

While *I* know that Tim Keller's words are true, I am not suggesting you should believe them...not just yet. 'Belief' requires a decision, and reaching a decision is a process rather than an event. I think that faith is a continuum that progresses from *seeker* to *believer* to *knower.* When Jesus called His disciples, He didn't say, "Come, trust Me." He said, "Come, *follow* Me." It is only by wading into deeper waters that a beginner comes to *trust* that he can swim. It is something of an *epiphany*--an exhilarating progression that can only be accomplished through personal experience.

> *Epiphany: a sudden intuitive perception or
> insight into the reality or essential meaning of
> something.*

Epiphanies—particularly spiritual ones—can be electrifying. To that end, here's hoping that you're more than a little "'shocked" by the time that you've finished these pages.

So that is my introduction. I hope that you're intrigued and inspired to read further. And don't feel obliged to read these chapters in numerical order. After contention 1, give a read through #8---or maybe even start with 8—it's a doozy! I've prayed many a night over the pages that follow. I hope you will consider these contentions in your heart...and with your head.

There is a tide in the affairs of men, which, taken at the flood, leads on to fortune. Omitted, the voyage of a man's life is bound in shallows and in misery. On such a full sea are we now afloat. And we must take the current when it serves...or settle for mediocrity in our ventures.

- William Shakespeare

A man's character is his destiny.

- Heraclitus of Ephesus

CHAPTER 1
THE LENS

When you're asking fact-based questions, it's not satisfying to get faith-based answers.

- Andy Stanley

For now we see through a glass, darkly...

- 1 Corinthians 13:12 (KJV)

Through a glass darkly is a peculiar phrase. It implies that we can't comprehend reality through the lens of personal experience. While such an expression might seem assertive in our hyper-sensitive culture, that doesn't make it untrue. Americans are taught from an early age that it is our birthright to 'grow up' to be whatever we want to be. To do what *we want* to do. And while this *can* be our personal truth...it is not necessarily *wise*.

When I was ten years old, I wanted to be a professional racing jockey. I really, *really* wanted to race horses. I had no doubt I could earn my place in the Kentucky Derby Winner's Circle —just give me the chance to train! But by the time I was thirteen years old...reality set in. I weighed

160 pounds. Racing jockeys are small. Really small—120 pounds at the max. So no matter *how* much I *wanted* to be a racing jockey...I was *never* going to be a very successful one. I simply weighed too much! No amount of dieting could possibly make a difference, because I was a big guy. My *desire* to be a jockey meant *nothing* in the face of the truth. Reality didn't *care* how I felt about horse racing...because 'reality' isn't a personality that *can* care. No matter what *I* wanted, there would never be a Kentucky Derby Winner's Circle moment for me.

It was while recalling that childhood obsession one afternoon that I began to consider what *I wanted* out of life...in contrast to the life that was *happening* for me.

An admission of candor at the outset: your author claims no insight into the heart of the Creator Of The Universe. The contentions in this book are the culmination of personal life experiences. It never occurred to me to write a book like this when I was in my 20's. I didn't have the experiences for such a project then. The concept for this book didn't begin to take form until the middle of my 56th year, while listening to a series titled *Who Needs God?* by Andy Stanley of North Point Community Church (NPCC). Andy's message inspired me to think about the way that life—*my* life, had been working out. I shared my ideas with guys in my NPCC men's group. The guys encouraged me and helped to sharpen my thoughts...into *contentions*. The contentions in this book are a collection of personal epiphanies, brought to fruition with the help of intentional friends, inspiration from my pastor, and---as I offer for your consideration...by the God of The Universe Himself.

The Thinker, by Rodin (Photo by R. D. Koncerak)

THE POINT AND THE CHALLENGE

Much of human culture—from artistic expression to scientific discovery, has been driven by an awareness of our lifespan. Emerging as astonished creatures out of primordial time, we humans have always pondered "*why*" and "*how*" we got to be *alive* here and *conscious* (aka self-aware) in the first place. It is *futility* that draws us to consider the eternal—the utter *bewilderment* of what this is all about!! How are we supposed to *live* this life to accomplish...whatever we're supposed to accomplish? *How do we win? What* do we win?

Our *awareness* that we will ultimately die brings a focus and an urgency to our days. A resolve to accomplish, a striving, a need to express love *now* rather than later. If you knew you were going to live forever, after all, why bother to get out of bed? (Neil deGrasse Tyson)

To quote the mathematician Archimedes (something I think everyone should do at least once 😄), the striving of life is the search for "a lever and a place to stand" so that we can move the world just a little while we're on it. I believe that describes our predicament fairly well. Why do we matter? How is it that we make a difference?

Our experiences and our environment bring us to accumulate opinions over time. And as a man's opinions drive his decisions, so do they also direct his steps. These opinions about our environment and ourselves form our *character*. Our *character is formed though the impression that we develop of ourselves.*

While we *want* to believe that we form our own opinions, this book argues that God designed us to recognize our dependence on something that is separate from ourselves. This book contends that God created us to recognize our dependence...upon *Him*.

For much of my life, I took comfort and (naïve) confidence in a belief that, *way down deep*, everybody has a similar sense of "right and wrong". About the big stuff--like murder and rape. About stealing and lying. I *believed* that, because I was experiencing the world in the only way that I knew: through an individualized lens. My lens. My. Personal. Truth.

I was raised in what I have come to appreciate was a privileged environment. Not because my family was wealthy, but because I was loved and I was protected. Never once as a child did I have reason to question the motives of adults in my circle. That foundation formed my opinion of grown-ups: responsible, caring, and for the most part, capable. My early years were stable and comfortable. Since those times, like many of us,

I have been shaken in a number of ways. My father passed away after a long, debilitating condition. I experienced a heartbreaking divorce. I learned that a parent's unconditional love for his children is not reciprocal. I was unfairly forced out of a lucrative opportunity early in my career. I know what it feels like to be forgiven…and to not be forgiven. Like all of us, I am not unique--but I *am the culmination of my experiences.*

Some of you can relate to my protected childhood. Others grew up in a world less sheltered than my own. In one way or another, if you have any age on you, the reality of this life has taught you some hard-learned, undesirable lessons. But *we're still here.* And…with a capacity and an interest to understand what happens next.

IF YOU KNOW YO' MOMMA LOVES YOU…YOU JUST KNOW!

Personal experience cannot be refuted. A bully can tell you that your momma doesn't love you. But if you know in your heart that she does, then it is possible to brush off the insult. While others will decide whether or not to *agree* with what you believe, *personal experience is our reality.* If you know your momma loves you…you just *know!* No one can shake you from that reality…'ceptin yo' momma! Philosophies have detractors and ideologies have their critics. People form opinions and make decisions all the time about what they will and won't accept as truth. But *there is no substitute for personal experience* in drawing one's personal conclusions. It is only through *experience* that I've come to realize that some things just aren't going to happen the way that I want them to---no matter how hard I kick or I fuss. No matter how many horses I mount. I have learned that approaching life in the way that I am wired—without a *focus*, leads to frustration, embarrassment and failure. What I *want* is not always available to me (an epiphany that we've all shared, eh?). This is not a fun learning for us. I have lifelong experience with *uh-oh's, oh my's*…and more than a few *that didn't turn out like I expecteds*. Maybe you can relate?

Mark Twain said *"It ain't what you don't know that can hurt you. It's what you know for sure that just ain't so!"* Testing truth is a powerful force in shaping what we know to be true.

In *The Cure*, John Lynch & Co. puts it this way:

> God has shown all of His cards, revealing breathtaking protection. He says, in essence, "What if I tell them who they are now? What if I take away any element of fear? What if I tell them I will always love them? That I love them right now, as much as I love my only Son?
>
> What if I tell them there are not logs of past offenses, of how little they pray, or how often they've let me down? What if I tell them they are actually righteous, right now? What if I tell them I'm wild about them?
>
> What if I tell them that, if I'm their Savior, they're going to heaven no matter what—it's a done deal? What if I tell them they have a new nature, that they are saints, not saved sinners? What if I tell them I actually live in them now, my love, power and nature at their disposal? What if I tell them they don't have to put on masks? That they don't need to pretend we're close?

With promises like that, why would you look for reasons *not* to believe? But it may be a little early for you to accept that just yet...because *He made you that way!*

> *When I was a child, I talked like a child, I thought like a child, I reasoned like a child. When I became a man, I put the ways of childhood behind me. For now we see only a reflection as in a mirror; then we shall see face to face. Now I know in part; then I shall know fully, even as I am fully known.*

> - 1 Corinthians 13:11–12 (NIV)

> *Asking the right questions takes as much skill as giving the right answers.*

> - Robert Half

CHAPTER 2 AND GROUP ONE
CONTENTIONS 1- 4
HOW YOU WERE BORN

You were born **into a situation** and **in a specific condition**.

1. **You were born without a value system**
2. **You were born a forgetful creature**
3. **You were born with a desire to indulge your self-interest**
4. **You were born into a fallen world**

> *Doubt is not a pleasant condition. But certainty is an absurd one.*
>
> - Voltaire

THE CONTENTIONS: FROM GOD IN THE FIRST PERSON

I made you the way that you are. I know why you behave in the ways that you do, why you react in the ways that you do, why you believe, pursue, rebel, create, and dream in all of the remarkable ways that you do. It's because of Me. I made you and I am proud of you.

You were born with a perception of My existence. This is not a choice that you have. How you *act* on your perception of Me, though, is entirely up to you. I created you with the ability *to make conscious choices*.

Now, every rule has its exceptions: If I have a particular purpose in mind for you (eg: Paul, Moses, Jonah, et al.), you will learn that at the appropriate time. Otherwise, you are *capable* of contemplating a variety of alternatives to avoid or explain Me away. But you will never be at peace if you are in denial about who I Am. Your existence will never entirely make sense without acknowledging Me. I know that this is true about you... because I Am the one who made you.

These pages contend that you cannot live your best life without Me. You were not created to live life on your terms, though I know that is surely your preference. I *know* that you don't like to be told what to do, and I surely know that you don't like to give up control. I Am the *only* one--besides you, who knows what's going on inside your head. I designed your bone marrow to make blood cells. I Am why you sway to a good beat. I gave you eyesight to marvel at a sunrise. Beer was my idea. I made sex feel good (you thought that happened by itself?). I designed you to *realize* through the course of your life...that you were created to have a relationship with Me. Angels dance when somebody recognizes who I Am—because it is *always* a joyful epiphany. And the day *will* come when you acknowledge me, too. Alive in this world or afterward...because I said so.

IN THE BEGINNING

The story of creation is actually very cool. I'm proud of how that all came together. It was a lot of work, and it was worth it.

I did it for you.

Adam and Eve and the apple on the tree has been moralized as a tale of self-indulgence. And it was. A self-righteous decision was made in a paradise that defied My specific instruction. It betrayed the fellowship I intended for you—and at the same time it exemplified who you are: a creation with the privilege to choose. You can think what you want about the consequences of Adam and Eve's choices, but they knew what they knew...and *they chose the decisions that they made.*

Eating from the tree of 'knowing good and evil' meant Adam and Eve were asserting authority *to do what was right in their eyes.* They were created to have authority over the earth. And they were your parents. The way that I made them--and you, is intense and absolute. *And* you are responsible to Me for your choices. That's what free will is about. You are awesome and you were born with an attitude.

But you were not created to *captain your soul* as that arrogant poem asserts. You make choices up to a point...and then those choices begin to make *you*.

Whether you believe the story of Eden or not—or if it even applies to you, it is worth considering what happens when you do what is 'right in your own eyes'....

CONTENTION 1: YOU WERE BORN WITHOUT A VALUE SYSTEM

Cultures change in ways that are both superficial and profound. When the essayist Joseph Epstein was young, he observed that when you went into the drugstore, the cigarettes were on the open shelves and the condoms were behind the counter. But now when you go to the drugstore the condoms are on the open shelves and the cigarettes are behind the counter.

- David Brooks, *The Road To Character*

For I am naturally formed to look after my own interest. If it is my interest to have an estate in land, it is my interest also to take it from my neighbor. If it is my interest to have a garment, it is my interest also to steal it from the bath. This is the origin of wars, civil commotions, tyrannies, conspiracies.

- Epictetus (AD 60–138), Discourses, Book 1

Stay with me through this paragraph:

You were not born with a cultural worldview...though you were certainly born *into* one. By 'cultural', I mean the evolving set of morals that people use to judge what is pleasing, what is hip, what is fashionable, what is 'right' and what is 'wrong'. You weren't hard-wired with opinions as an infant—though you surely recognized comfort and sustenance. While you had drives and passions, you had little use for social norms beyond how you felt about facial hair or a wet diaper! Where morals are concerned, you were born a blank slate. All of the opinions that are wadded up inside you have evolved through the spectacle of your life experience. Your opinions and value system are unique. Your 'free will' has constructed your value system. By the time you reached adulthood, your conscience had accumulated a variety of experiences. And your basis for interpreting those experiences has become your assembled worldview. This is the "lens" through which you navigate the world around you. *Every* person has his or her own unique lens. Just like snowflakes. God does stuff like that ☺).

Make sense? I hoped so. Read on.

As a child, you adopted much of your parents' lens (or that of whatever adult presence was around you) and you interpreted your world much as they did. Their 'rights' and their 'wrongs' became your right and wrong...because that was the world that you knew. As you matured, however, you came to realize that *choice* in itself is a privilege. You began to consider for *yourself* what was appealing—and you established the beginnings of a value system that was your own. While that value system started as an adoption of family norms, the *lens* you crafted to evaluate your environment was becoming uniquely and spectacularly *yours.* Your decisions. Your choices and challenges. *Now how cool is that?* Or it certainly seemed so at the time.

Now, the process of developing your personal value system was surely fraught with twists and turns. As a teenager, you experimented with different value systems—sometimes as often as you changed socks. Your sexual awakening played a part in that. Boy, did it ever. While the adults in your life had provided the foundation, *you refined your value system as the outcomes of your decisions warranted.* Read that sentence again. It is the essence of being human. You have the capacity to choose, and you incorporate choices into your lens as the pageant of life unfolds. *The focus that powers the choices you make will determine the course of your life.* Read that sentence again, too.

For example, you were not born with a work ethic, though the nobility of labor is pretty much universally celebrated. To be engaged as a laborer shows the world that you are profitable to someone—worthy of being chosen and set to a task. It is easier to not envy or steal when your stomach is full, and when your family is clothed and sheltered. Enablement and labor provide a purpose. Labor keeps a man physically and psychologically healthy. Entitlement does the opposite. Entitlement does not foster gratitude…it fosters resentment. But unless the behaviors of a work ethic: getting up in the morning and arriving at the job on time, cooperating with others, deference to superiors, respect for authority and the conventions of personal appearance—were modeled for you in youth, you may have had a rough time adopting these behaviors on your own. And so to some degree, you did (or you didn't). Perhaps you learned the 'right' ways and the 'wrong' ways to approach a job interview. Hired is good. Fired is bad. It is hard to *per*form until you've learned to *con*form to the conventions and the practices of your culture. These are decisions you must make, but your *view* of them—your formative lens, was modeled by examples observed in youth.

Throughout human history, "right and wrong" has meant a lot of different things. To believe that civilizations through time have acknowledged even a *similar* sense of "right and wrong" is a serious misconception of the truth. There was nothing in the DNA that brought you into this world that instilled in you a sense of right and wrong. You were not born with a moral compass, and there is no such thing as a morality common to humankind.

Now, before you hit your mental reject button, know this: Contention #1 has polled as the most *contentious* contention among the twelve. A compelling case is offered on the pages that follow, and I ask your forbearance to read it in full before forming an opinion (hat tip to John Pearson).

Consider the cultures that prevailed before the time of Jesus. Molech is (unfortunately) a good example. Molech was a big deal in his day. He was a god of the Canaanites and nearby peoples that required the burning blood of children to keep him happy. Baby's blood. Supplied regularly. With fire. Infants were tossed alive onto the glowing hands of a bronze statue...and suffered what today would be decried as a horrific death. But fidelity to Molech was *truth* in the eyes of the Canaanites. It was a righteous practice in their eyes. To them it was genuinely...*honorable.*

A depiction of Molech
(From the 1897 *Bible Pictures and What They Teach Us* by Charles Foster).

Throughout Asian and Mesoamerican history, sex rituals have been important for the pleasing of gods and their acolytes. Obligatory sex (a novel word pairing!) rituals have been practiced across generations of "good and upstanding" citizens—because their cultural belief system expected it of them.

In pretty much every *non-Christian* civilization since the beginning of time, *men* have been in charge, *women* have been property...and that has essentially been that. In Old Testament Israel, David wrote fervently of "striking down women and children—spare not even their livestock from the sword!" Really. That was the *culture* they knew—the *value system* that people navigated in that day. Such was the prevailing societal lens at that particular time in history. In the "truth" of their day, Molech demanded infant blood... Aphrodite and Ishtar required sex. That was the cultural truth.

Now, did *every* person ascribe to these (unsettling) conventions? No, because *morality is personal when truth is personal*. But the *conventions* of that day most certainly influenced the behavior of *most* citizens much of the time. Lifetime after lifetime...after lifetime. That's where human history comes from. Icky, huh?

Self-righteous civilizations don't practice a common morality. They *create* it, enhance it, make it up by their very selves, and evolve it to suit their purposes. When championed by those with influence, leaders of a particular brand of morality attract followers. Commonfolk are coopted by practices that seem advantageous. *Let's all just try to get along!* Practice becomes custom, custom becomes belief, and belief gives way... to allegiance. When believers come to power, doubters are marginalized, humiliated. Objectors are chastised and nonconformers are outcasts. Banished, imprisoned, or worse. After all, nonconformers are dangerous, racist, intolerant and prejudiced, right? Nonconformers present an opposition. An offense. What makes you think that *you're* so special? Nonconformers should be sacrificed on the pyres of their resistance, no?

And don't limit yourself to abominations (please!). Left to human devices, mindsets about marriage, employment, property rights and *fairness*...are intricately tied to *culture*— the faint and tender time frame during which you are reading these words. With merely a shift in the winds of popularity, morality yields to the breeze. This should be unsettling to you.

For the record, there has never been a "Christian" nation--only Christian *persons*. Frank Peretti refers to these as "the remnant" and I like that term. I have watched a parade of peoples preen across the stage of history. Honestly, you've proven remarkably consistent to the way that I designed you. I wish that you could see this through My *lens*, so to speak. I so dearly want you to embrace My vision of human dignity. But it's *your* choice.

THE EVOLUTION OF DIGNITY

The Romans and Greeks were among the first (that we know of) to incorporate a dignity to citizenship. But that dignity was defined by privilege—and not by right. As far as the *dignity of life* was concerned, the Greeks were a brutal culture. The Romans were worse.

When a Roman father wasn't charmed by his newborn baby—because she was a girl, perhaps, because the poor creature was deformed or the timing of child birth was inopportune, that father could "expose" the tender infant to the elements (to die)…and suffer no consequence. No guilt, no remorse, because the choice for that life was *his privilege*. That was the practice of the Romans and Greeks…it was their *truth*. Leave that little baby by the river to die…and go about tending the yardwork. What fate would befall the baby didn't factor in the formula that determined a *family*. Only the father's acceptance mattered. That. Was. Their. Personal. Truth.

> *In both Greece and Rome, children's lives had little value, and a father's rights included killing his own children. The proportion of men greatly exceeding that of women…suggesting that girls suffered infanticide more often than boys. A kind of social birth, the ritual right to survive, rested on the procedure of name-giving in the Roman culture and on the start of oral feeding in the Germanic tradition. Legislative efforts to protect the newborn began with Emperor Trajan in 103 A.D. and Constantine following his conversion to Christianity in 313 A.D. Mal-formed newborns were not regarded as human and were usually killed immediately after birth. Infanticide was outlawed in 374 A.D. by Emperor Valentinian.*
>
> - M. Obladen – From *Right to Sin*: Laws on Infanticide in Antiquity, 2015 abstract (reprinted from PubMed.gov)

And then came Jesus.

> *Christianity elevated the individual soul against*
> *impossible odds.*
>
>   - Jordan Peterson

The ideals that Jesus introduced to the world were nothing short or radical: the sanctity of human life, uniform morality, kindness for the downtrodden---and the weekend!! (Shabbat came from the Jews – look it up).

There is neither Jew or Gentile, neither slave nor free, nor is there male or female Gal 3:28 (NIV). This was indeed revolutionary.

Early Christians earned a reputation for saving abandoned babies. It was a practice that distinguished them as unconventional…and dangerous. After all, if you were a self-respecting patriarch who'd decided that your baby should die…only to learn that some *Christian* had rescued the child and *embraced* the infant as a blessing from God…well… that was scandal and an outrage! Was it a god's will that brought such a disruptive outcome…or was it an annoying intervention by non-conformists?

Cultures established with a Judeo-Christian heritage function differently from those founded otherwise. Doubt this? Try living under sharia law for a while…or under any form of government-by-command. Try practicing your "liberty" in Malaysia or Saudi Arabia. An undisciplined American would not last long on the streets of Indonesia. Or Pakistan. Their practices and norms…their societal *truths*, are vastly different from truths that Westerners know. Offend in a strange culture…and they'll put you in jail. And some countries might just behead you. There is no appeal. Your opinion about consequence doesn't matter outside of your culture.

Now to be practical, gentle reader, if you live in Ohio, odds are that you won't involuntarily visit Pakistan. But if you transported your Ohio 'lens' to an unfamiliar society, my point is that your opinions could get you in trouble. Particularly if you assert your Western "rights." You *can* be sincere...and yet be sincerely *wrong* about how things will work out. Communities are more barbarous than individuals, and less likely to tolerate aliens. Nonconformers are typically eyed with suspicion...and in history they were once fed to lions. For entertainment. Audiences cheered.

Jesus's teaching allegorized the bleeding Samaritan in a ditch. Under Jewish law, women were *property*. Like a goat. Or a shoe. A culture-conforming Jew wouldn't conceive of engaging a leper...and not just because of disease. Far worse: a person with leprosy was unclean. They were *lesser beings* who were suffering the penalty of their sin (just like AIDS, right?). They were suffering what they *deserved*—it was their station in life, and one was best to leave them to it. It was Jesus who took those sorry sinners by the hand— *for the first time in history*...and spoke with them. Dined with them. He healed them. It was astonishing. Peculiar. Outrageous.

In the ancient world, everybody was a potential slave for somebody (Stanley). But into that world, the apostle Paul held forth that men and women had *equal* standing and should be respectful of one another. "Joint heirs" he said.

This was novel. This was new. It had *never* before been asserted to humankind. It was something new under the sun.

The gods of pre-Christian cultures *didn't care* how you treated other people. The rules regarded only how *they* were to be treated. The gods of some Middle Eastern cultures don't care much how you treat each other *today*. But when Jesus came along, He told us that we are accountable to one another. That we should *love* one another...just as He loves us. This was a first. Have I made my point?

Jesus dined with corrupt officials. He showed respect to prostitutes. Such principles, while unevenly deployed, are *foundational* to Western culture. Regardless of how you acknowledge Him, it was Jesus who introduced these principles to humankind.

Within a few short years of demonstrating these astonishments, the fabric of Roman culture disintegrated. Their entire societal structure came undone. How about that?

That God *made* us to resonate in the presence of noble conventions is undeniable. How surprising should it be that we recognize our better selves in His example? In Lincoln's words, that we would *serve the better angels of our nature?*

Once you see something, you cannot unsee it. But what you see depends upon your lens. Personal truth can be argued. It can be denied. In the 1500s, you could be burned at the stake for denying that Earth was the center of the universe— by so-called 'learned' bishops! But this is the point: when introduced as The Way, The Truth and The Life, the truths of Jesus profoundly affected the human societal lens. Just sayin'.

The soul is dyed by the color of your thoughts.

- Marcus Aurelius

If you think all this is in the past, that evolving morality isn't so much an issue in *our* time, go to your browser and type in "eugenics" or "red scare". There are Americans still alive (in 2023) who celebrated at "negro lynchings". The cultural truths that command our attention today bear no resemblance to what consumed us a mere fifty years ago. Human slavery is not an event of history. Neither is female genital mutilation. Or cannibalism. They exist---and to a degree that would shock most Americans. The Rohingya tragedy in Southeast Asia is a contemporary holocaust. Check out Isis Chang's *The Rape of Nanking* or type "Japan Unit 731" into your browser. It will (should) make you sick. I can go on: the so-called killing fields of the Khmer Rouge, and the brutal gulags of the Soviet era. Examples horrendously abound. Without Jesus, our opinions about rape, racial equality and the dignity of human life are merely 'pop culture'. It is *Christian* culture that is at war these days with the abominable sex trafficking industry. Evil is real, and it is near. Just sayin'.

Rohingya refugees near the Balukali camp
in Cox's Bazar, Bangledesh, in 2017. PHOTO:
KEVIN FRAYER, GETTY IMAGES

Only man will inflict suffering for the sake of suffering. That is the best definition of evil I have been able to formulate. Only man could conceive of the rack, the iron maiden and the thumbscrew.

- Jordan Peterson

There are no small contentions in these pages.

Your author was born in 1961. *Nobody* who held elected office back then was advocating LGBTQ+ lifestyles...let alone celebrating such behaviors with parades. No court in 1961 could fathom that taxpayers should fund a woman's right "to choose"...let alone pay for gender transitioning. TV networks in the 1960's censored the slightest "blue" inference. Homosexuality was generally regarded as "icky" in 1973...but that's when *Rowe v. Wade* became law.

Gender-affirming surgery barely existed 1979...when a gay rights march in Washington, DC drew 125,000 participants. I recall listening to Peter Jennings on the *ABC Nightly News* comparing the gay rights march to the 30,000 Ku Klux Klan members who marched on those same streets in 1925... wearing white robes and pointy hoods. In 2014, President Obama signed Executive Order 13672, adding "gender identity" and "sexual orientation" to categories protected from discrimination in the federal civilian workforce. Some state governments now pay for "medically necessary" gender transition-related surgery. How's *that* for an evolution of tolerance---if not truth, across just my lifetime?

> *We live not only our own lives but, whether we know it or not, we also live the life of our time. We are all making history together, we are part of an era, and we are responsible to each other in this great project.*
>
> - Laurens van der Post

I wish I had a cool name like that.

I graduated from high school in 1979. China's "one child" policy was announced that same year. By 1990, if estimates are correct, that "policy" had prevented or *terminated* 300 million births. 300 million. In 11 years. A figure that approaches the population of the United States. The consequence of Deng Xiaoping's *policy* is profound. Russia invades the Ukraine...because they can. These are realities that are happening in our lifetimes. This is the cultural reality.

THE GRAVITY OF IT ALL

We live in an age where we choose to believe that opinion is our rightful reality. That there is no such thing as truth that is uniform at all times, in all places and for all peoples. That the reality of others doesn't apply to us. So says us.

I remember debating this subject at a university in Kiev in 2005. A roomful of enlightened Eastern European students were questioning (scoffing, really…) at my naïve contention of "absolute truth". We were meeting in a classically beautiful conference room, with floor-to-ceiling windows and an ornate piano positioned in one corner. I referred to the piano to make a point:

"I invite any one of you", I dared and pointed, "to take the stairs, walk outside and position yourself directly beneath this window. I, in turn, am going to shove this piano out through the glass and send it careening down onto your head. You may *choose* to believe that this piano won't hit you. You can believe it with all your might. Anger can well up inside of you, you can shake your fists and scream at the top of your lungs that *it's not fair* that this piano is going to hit you. But my contention is this: the piano won't care. It won't care how you feel about it crushing you… because it can't. You will *absolutely* be squished (or so I contend!)--whether you *choose* to believe it or not. You may not care for that reality…but truth has no *capacity for opinion*". Eyebrows were wiggling as I observed their features and words. I'm pretty sure those were Ukrainian expletives.

Thank goodness---I suggest for your consideration, that the God of Truth *cares*!

You can sincerely believe that your truth is reality... because you *can* be sincerely *wrong*. Your nature is to want truth to be personal—whatever free will arouses you to pursue. That is your inborn preference--because I made you that way. You were made with a will to command your destiny. I put that yearning in your heart. It's the spark of Me that empowers you. "In My image", so to speak. When you acknowledge Me, your heart will be pricked to discern the truth that you were created for. Free will enables you to command your choices, but it also commands you to choose.

Recognizing that you were born without a value system is not a poverty. You alone in My creation can contemplate what is good and what is evil. It is the capacity for you to know, above all, that I Am good. It is your nature to be curious and to ponder this reality. Take care, dear child, that you do not lift up your soul to what is false. You were created to wonder who I Am, and to sense Me in your heart. I made you that way.

CONTENTION 2: YOU ARE AN ASTONISHINGLY FORGETFUL CREATURE

My mind works like lightning. One brilliant flash and it's gone.

- George Burns

Not to brag, but I just went into another room and actually remembered why I went in there. It was the bathroom, but still …

- Facebook post

There are more than 100 billion neurons in the human brain, of which only 15 percent appear to be activated. There are more connections in the human body than there are stars in the galaxy. We possess a gigantic network of information to which we have almost no access.

- Morgan Freeman, quoted from the film Lucy, *Universal Pictures 2014*

This is a short one, because you'll remember it better if it's brief ☺.

You retain little in memory of what you experience throughout a given day. What you *do* recall is subject to bewildering distortion. The day before yesterday? Fuggedaboutit. You are prone to altered memories, to distraction from plans, and to abandon your projects half-finished. Is that chuckling I hear? Thought so. Even *how* you remember things is subject to change over time—affected by mood, health, and your environment. Obligations in our lives require discipline and resolve…qualities not common to humankind! But cut yourself some slack when it comes to this contention...'cause there's a lot to keep up with in any given day! Throw an occasional crisis into the affairs of daily living, and recollections quickly become unstable.

It's an interesting fact of self-awareness, don't you think? We *recognize* that memory is a fickle thing. We *know* that this is our nature. Can you imagine that rabbits consider such things? Do you think that elephants do? As far as we know, this self-awareness is unique to humankind. I contend that God made us this way.

And because we *know* such things about ourselves—because we *know* that we're prone to forgetfulness, our minds continually seek points of reference to navigate our daily affairs. Points of reference that validate our worldview, using our chosen lens. Our lives are defined by our memories and our experiences, but we are more *stream-of-consciousness* creatures than we are a reservoir (or a puddle) of recollections.

This is a big deal, and it's an important issue to wrestle with. Why? Because this: once you realize that you are prone to a shifting sense of what is true (Contention 1), forgetfulness (instability) should assume a certain urgency. If what is important today becomes less so tomorrow, is that because we *did* something, *experienced* something...or *ate* something that changed our priorities? If what was true in your life yesterday is less true today, is that a good thing? Emotion can play a big part. Medications like Ritalin and Adderall are widely (hugely!) prescribed to focus attention and recall in our society. It's an unsettling element of our condition—and it is magnified by the demands of our culture. (Is Ritalin a chicken or an egg thing?)

If considering this condition is disturbing to you, go easy on yourself. There is nothing wrong with a little self-examination---so long as you consider next what to *do* about it! Because there is a reason for this condition. You were made this way. This fantastic condition confirms our need for a dependable, unchanging point of reference. This condition is the platform...for *epiphany*.

Some Christians call it "conversion", but *epiphany* has always seemed a better word to me, as it describes an *inspired truth* about our condition. "Oh, *that's* why! Oh, so *that's* how it works! This book contends that you can't "do life" on your own very well...*because God designed you to be sensitive to His truth*. This insight may come to you as a tap on the shoulder, a whisper in your ear...or a body blow that knocks you off a horse (that had to hurt, Saul!). Indeed, you were *created* for this epiphany during your lifetime. I contend that *it is essential to the human condition.* Evangelicals sometimes use the term *conviction* for a person feeling pressure to Believe. 'Conviction' in this sense is not related to condemnation, but instead it is the means for *connection*.

Without Me as your foundation of truth—your solid ground, you are prone to be influenced by the opinions and the immediacy of what surrounds you: your friends, YouTube channels and your culture. Without a truth that is separate from you, a truth that enforces you, your fading memories leave you prone to the quirks of your culture. Emotions move in and out like weather systems. They are temporary.

When a personal experience becomes a part of your lens, it is quite a troubling matter to "un-know" it (remember - your momma loves you!) *Un-knowing* is not the same as forgetting. You forget stuff all the time. But you *can* turn away from what you know to be true—that's what free will is all about. You can deny it, you can refute it, or find workarounds to accommodate a different life path. But your obstinance does not affect the truth. That is why free will is such a breathtaking thing. One can insist that *truth* is a personal matter…but *truth* has no regard for your opinion. "Personal truth" is the narcissist's way to redefine *opinion*.

It would be nice if "solid ground" was all that is required. Find a church, join a bible study, and pursue Christian fellowship. But a church is a congregation…of people. Insular, guarded, doctrinal, absolutist, judgmental, fickle…people. A lot of doctrinal Christians know what is right…in their own eyes. Drinking is bad…while gluttony is rarely discussed. Divorce is an abomination…but stigmatizing and shunning those who suffer it is righteous indignation. Our capacity for sanctimony seemingly has no bounds. Congregations, too, are subject to shifting priorities…but can leave in their wake the frustrated, dejected, defeated and abandoned—who may ultimately turn away from "organized religion" (deny, refute). What felt protective for a time became confining…stale…and at last irrelevant.

And even still…and ever after, *you remain prone to ask. And prone to wonder.* And that's OK. Because. I. Am. Still. Here.

Let's be clear about something: I am God. I never promised to *convince* you—to pound you over the head about who I Am. I am not here to accept your dares or to drop amazing miracles at your command.

You have circumstances to deal with, and that's your lot. You live in a fallen world (more on that later). I am not here to give you what you want when you want it. That would make *you* god. I *Am* here when you call out to me, to remind you that I Am willing to accept you as you are, and I Am open to show you truth as you pursue Me. That's the way it works...because I said so.

The habits of making Christian fellowship part of your life, of considering and testing a pastor's teachings, of reading supportive Christian literature—those are activities that *reinforce* a forgetful mind and *strengthen* an unstable value system. You need those things. The fruit of such pursuits...is peace. Life in a fellowship will enable you to contribute when you are able and to draw strength when you are weak and vulnerable. That's why the bible is such an important part of Christian life--because the words of faithful translations won't change—regardless of age or circumstance. It is the consistency of that unchanging text that can anchor your faith and transcend culture. As such, it can be immeasurably reassuring.

Prayer is reinforcement. It reinforces *us*. Prayer can be contrition, adoration, confession, intercession, thanksgiving— all affirmations and reminders of who God is, and of who we are in relationship to Him. The human ability to pray is one of God's most spectacular, life-changing gifts. We have *constant access* to the eternal God of the universe. And what you do with this privilege...is entirely up to you. Wow.

People who feel trapped in a stressful relationship or who have suffered significant loss often throw themselves into a distraction or life change. They do this to alter their circumstances and get their mind off what is hurting them. It works. Changing jobs, moving to a new place, buying a fixer-upper, or even indulging in yard work can be cathartic. And doing this changes the priority of our limited attention span. Problems, relationships—even feelings for close family members can fade when the mind is consumed with deliberate disruptions and distractions.

There are plenty of examples how focus shields our attention from other things—no matter how obvious they might seem. Dr. Daniel Simons's famous study of selective attention featured an "invisible gorilla" waltzing across a stage. Type "Daniel Simons invisible gorilla" into your browser to check it out. It's compelling.

Here is another classic illustration that demonstrates priority and concentration: the more we focus on a single thing, the more other stuff will fade in comparison. It is not just your memory that fades...it's your *limited capacity* to maintain a broader view. That's because the 'lens' that you adopt is self-reinforcing. So be careful what you choose to be focused on and what you pursue to reinforce it.

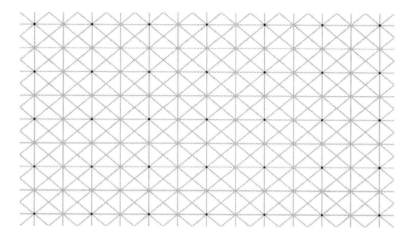

There are 35 dots within the intersections of the boxes above. It is impossible to see more than a few dots at a time as your eyes focus on various parts of the diagram. There is a limit to your capacity to focus and prioritize. By focusing on one dot, you can actually *make* other dots disappear! When you focus on one thing, other things—*no matter how precious*, will fade from view. This is a serious truth: you cannot see all of what is right in front of you. God made you that way.

CONTENTION 3: YOU ARE DRAWN TO INDULGE YOUR SELF-INTEREST

> *What is it you plan to do with your one wild and precious life?*
>
> - Mary Oliver

This one may seem obvious--but that's the point. It is hard to deny that *you* are the center of your universe. *Your* opinions, *your* thoughts, *your* desires, *your* lens. You love your family and your circle of friends. Or *you* don't. You are *not* continually drawn to help those outside your circles or to address another's needs before your own needs have been met. Should you happen upon a stranger in crisis, *perhaps* you are inclined to intervene—at least to call for help! But in doing so, you can come to your fill of it quickly. Generosity satisfies us, inspires us. But putting another ahead of ourselves is *inconvenient*. It's exceptional--or perhaps it is a *concession*. Handing a homeless guy five bucks is a magnanimous demonstration of generosity, right? How kind of *me*—how noble! We feel validated for accommodating 'the better angels of our nature'. But should a second beggar or *third* one approach in succession…well, this is just too much! It ruins the moment! Perhaps it even gets on your nerves! *Why is that?* Why is it that unless the motivation suits *our* interest (Is this tax deductible? Social media post-worthy?), our generosity reaches a limit once we've satisfied *our* desire to contribute. We pursue things that indulge *our* self-interest.

Now don't go getting offended. (you can *feel* that inside, huh?). It is *natural to pursue our self-interest*. To desire things that make ourselves happy. Palming 5-spots to homeless guys is unsettling. Far worse if it's a woman who is asking!

It's uncomfortable, it's awkward. You don't want them (her!) to be there. We *don't want* that to exist. We don't like our sensibilities to be invaded. Without a higher purpose, our intentions are really quite...selfish.

That tendency to be selfish is accompanied by... *temptation*. Pursuing what is right in your own eyes. What feels good. What looks good. It's a tree-of-good-and-evil thing. They ate it, you got it. All sorts of evil can emerge from self-indulgence. It's what causes you to reach for the apple.

You were born with the challenge to contend with this nature. To find order in pursuit of your wants. To find a compass that orients your purpose and meaning—to orient what you know to be *true*. That pursuit inside of you is the drive to find...Me. I put that there. It is the drive to understand the nature of your desires—*the nature of who you are*. You are too fantastic a creature to just have evolved from primordial goo. You know this. But without Me, you can't imagine how it happened.

The phrase "You be you" is a popular cultural embrace. The 1960's version was "If it feels good, do it". After you've tried that on for a while, though, you realize that not everyone embraces you the same. That approach to life stands quite in opposition to "Be holy as I Am holy". Just sayin'.

So what about the guy in Mongolia, you ask, who lived in 1400 BC and could not possibly have heard about Abraham? Or Jesus? What *truth* could that guy have possibly known?

While that is a reasonable (and common) question, it is framed in a limited perspective. After all, if Jesus was born at a specific time and in a specific place to fulfill a specific set of prophecies (according to the bible), then He did what He did for a reason...and that reason was not to bring *entitlement* to all of mankind. Should everyone everywhere be *entitled* to *your* understanding of salvation? Should we all have equal opportunity to "get God" or "have God" in the way that we are drawn to know Him in our time? Shouldn't we get to acknowledge God in a way that suits *our* sense of fairness? How's *that* for a dose of "social justice!"

Dear reader, you think too much of yourself if you believe that you can "choose God". The truth is, and will *only* ever be, that God is holding on to *you*. With an invitation, with an expectation and with an all-powerful, all-encompassing experience: a profound truth is that you are witnessing life through the very eyeballs that God designed for you to use. Your physical, genuine *lens*. Until you stop believing that life is all about you, a man or woman will never begin to appreciate the astounding, spectacular miracle of conscious creation.

In *The Songs of Jesus*, Timothy Keller writes that God's Word keeps us from being deceived about who we are, as well as from being a deceiver of others. "Contemporary people", he writes, "tend to examine the bible...for things that they cannot accept. But Christians should reverse that, allowing the bible to examine us, looking for things God cannot accept. The psalmist sets about being faithful to God's laws. We can't truly understand scripture unless we make a basic commitment...". This is a responsibility that can only happen after *epiphany*.

Jesus didn't first invite His disciples to *believe* Him...He asked only that they *follow* Him. Belief develops through personal experience.

> *Walk into any large mall, museum, amusement park, university, or hospital, and you will typically meet at once a very large map with the famous red star and the encouraging words "You Are Here". These maps are offered to visitors as a way to orient themselves to their situation, get some perspective on things. This is the Big Picture. This is where you are in that picture. Hopefully you now know where to go. You have your bearings.*
>
> *Oh, that we had something like this for our lives. This is the Story in which you have found yourself. Here is how it got started. Here is where it went wrong. Here is what will happen next. Now this-this is the role you've been given. If you want to fulfill your destiny, this is what you must do. These are your cues. And here is how things are going to turn out in the end.*
>
> *We can".*
>
> - John Eldredge, *Epic*

Plenty of books have been written and movies made on the premise that *there is a warrior inside of you*. Pursuit of an honor that is *bigger than you* strikes a chord in every man's heart. If you're a man reading this, you feel a stirring at just the thought of it. Inspiring, right? There are manly passions aroused in the presence of honor, bravery and benevolence.

Of course there is a warrior inside of you. I designed you to *want* to take command. With inspiration, you *can* be brave and will readily sacrifice for others. I did that, and I admire that about you.

Temptation, on the other hand, is the desire to pursue your self-interest. There are *plenty* of temptations that are *good* for you. Excellent, in fact. But temptations are driven for *your* satisfaction and *not* for the betterment of *others*. Not for the glory of Me. Interesting, huh? When satan tempted Jesus, they *both knew better.* They both knew how the encounter was going to work out...but they were drawn to their roles nonetheless. They both had spiritual histories. And yet Jesus was feeling what is common in man... because I made man that way.

You're never going to be content down here. You were not made to be so. Are you sensing a theme here? And that brings us to the next point...

CONTENTION 4: YOU LIVE IN A FALLEN WORLD

*He has made everything beautiful in its time.
He has also set eternity in the human heart; yet
no one can fathom what God has done from
beginning to end.*

- Ecclesiastes 3:11 (NIV)

So how you doin' so far?

If you're like most folks—and if you've been evaluating the
reality of your circumstance through these words—then the
limits of your nature are becoming apparent. Indeed, the
more you are willing to consider that your behaviors were
intentionally *designed*, the closer you are to appreciating
that the desires of this world are, well…*worldly.* Your *nature*
doesn't suit this reality. The truth is that *this is not the world
in which you were created to live.*

**That story at the beginning of Genesis—"the fall
of man" and all that, set the table for your curious
condition. It was inborn rebellion that got you
where you are (another contention), but you have
a spark of Me in you. It's what Christians refer to
as the *sanctity* of of human life. It is your innate
dignity. I designed you to *know* who you are—and
to aspire to what you *should* be. That's where those
feelings of *entitlement* come from. They come from
Me. Your *knowing* that you are special…is actually a
very special thing. When you're thinking that your
life is not "fair", that's because you're thinking
about reality through *your* eyes. Through the lens *I*
gave you. Until that entitled lens of yours is focused**

on Me...it will *search* for what you think might be worthy. You will compare your situation to that of other people. But you *are* special. You *are* unique. You are gifted, and you are loved—and that is *the truth* about who you are.

Without My perspective, you will remain myopic, focusing on small things. And you will remain immature. Maturity requires both focus and experience to realize what is beyond yourself. Outside of yourself. Though you will always be *capable* of redemption, staying narrow-minded makes you a wretched human being. At some level, you *know* this is not your world. You know that you were *made* for better. That you *deserve* better—whether or not you are comfortable even admitting it. You have the *capacity* to broaden your gaze. *That* is the eternity that is set inside your heart.

Your sanctity is why I let humanity live through the Great Flood thing. Your ancestors were pathetic, and I was angry. I actually wondered for a time if this *exercise by epiphany* was worth the frustration. I vented on account of their obstinance, and it was terrible. It is heartbreaking when your children make bad choices. Over and over. But I decided that you *are* worth it. That you *are* entitled. So whether or not you know it, you were *born* lucky. You *alone* have the privilege to rely on Me. To acknowledge Me as the One who can complete you. And that choice has greater purpose than you may know...

THE MEANING OF LIFE

The showcase of humanity—and your innate sense of eternity, demonstrates to all of heaven that *you were designed with an instinct to recognize your Creator*. I made you--and all the creatures of heaven that way, too. It was rebellion up Here that made it necessary to create you as an *example* for heaven to witness. A *demonstration* that an existence viewed through *any other lens* cannot complete what is true. That is truth for you—and it's truth for the angels Here in heaven. It is how you become *fully known* and how you come to know that you are fully *loved*.

That ability to *choose* is a privileged and dangerous gift. It is the gift on which all humanity turns. It is quite the drama to watch you from up Here. *You*, in fact, are the top-rated show since creation began! All the world truly is a stage. And men and women really *are* players. How about *that*, Shakespeare?

There is a footnote in my bible at the bottom of Ecclesiastes 3—the verse at the front of this chapter. Referencing *"He also set eternity in the human heart"*, the footnote offers an alternate translation: *"He placed ignorance in the human heart, so that..."*. Like the "through a glass darkly" theme that runs through the Old and New Testaments, biblical authors write that we (as mere mortals) can't get our heads around the purpose and the meaning of life—though we are *certainly* drawn to contemplate it. To feel responsible in how we approach life. Whether you feel thwarted by design or limited by IQ will determine how you evaluate that biblical footnote. Translation is an imprecise business, and responsibility is an adult sport.

Author Stephen Covey famously parsed *responsibility* as "the *ability* to *choose* your response". To Covey's way of thinking, *responsibility* means that you are *capable* of evaluating circumstances through your lens prior to taking action. To re*spond* rather than to re*act*. To contend otherwise--that you are *unable* to control your reaction to stimuli...is to say that you are *ir*responsible—or incapable of controlling your response. Not flattering! That you cannot control your outrage when the dog pees on the carpet, or when your spouse forgets to pay the mortgage. Covey's contention is that a *reaction*—like flinching at a pin prick or squinting your eyes when you sneeze--is uncontrollable. Reactions are different from responses. The point is that you have *two* levels of processing: an inborn hard-wiring that *reacts* to situations...and the *considered* ability to *respond*. So far as we know, man is the only creature that can distinguish between these two conditions. And as Andy Stanley says, "*You are far more likely to regret a reaction than to regret a response*". It's hard to argue with a statement like that when you consider your experiences with one and the other!

In Christian circles, attaining the ability to distinguish between reaction and response is termed *the age of responsibility*—the ability to discern "right" from "wrong." In criminal courts, the age of responsibility is generally a defendant's 18th birthday - the age at which one can be tried as an adult. Ughh. So much for maturity. Back to God:

It's been interesting to watch this creation unfold, to observe your groping *through a glass darkly*. There is an opinion among some of you that I am responsible for everything: bad things, good things, fortune and plagues. But here is My answer to that: just because I know *what* is going to happen, *when* something is going to happen and *how* you are going to respond,

how does this make *your* circumstance *My* fault? Why is it you curse Me when I don't intervene, but instead allow you to be *responsible*--as you were created to be? *My knowing in advance what you are going to do does not make your choices My fault.* Yes, you have tendencies, and you *are* predictable—that's what this book is about. But I made you self-aware and with the destiny to choose. So don't blame *Me* for your choices! You were made to know better. Mental illness, birth defects, disease, child abuse? Nobody signs up for those things. But those things happen in a fallen world.

Any number of bible verses intimate that *since the beginning of the world, there has been a plan for you.* If that is true (and it is), then consider how compelled and determined I must be to draw you in, to have you embrace My reality. Consider the pain, the suffering, the hatred, the disappointment and frustration I've witnessed and endured---generation after generation after generation. The heraldry, the victories, the disappointments, the irony---*just to prove out My point for those who follow Me.* And I didn't say *believe* Me. I said *follow Me.* Belief carries the benefit of experience. That is what heaven is watching from up Here. Sometimes it is beautiful. Sometimes it is gruesome.

Your struggle with Me is the singular adventure of your lifetime. I will abide all your suffering and pain—I will be ruthless and terrifying (that *sinner in the hands of an angry god* thing)—when I choose to, so to demonstrate to the remnant of heaven what your *choice* enables—and what choosing *truly* means for the created.

Just humble yourself and ask Me to show you who I Am. You'll get an answer. You decide what to do with it. That is how this works.

Make no mistake: I hold the cards. You *will* choose Me if I want you to. As with Saul, I enjoy Me some good self-correction. I have a great sense of humor. I invented the sense of humor! But unless I say so, it is *you* who does the choosing.

The grand point of living in a fallen world—the Meaning of Life, so to speak-- is that you are indeed an example. You will either engender the applause of heaven, or merit its eternal pity. I love you and I am uniquely aware of the incredible capacity that's within you. And I am *always* optimistic about your choice. But you live in a fallen world. *Adam* made you that way. Not My fault.

> *What if your blessings come through raindrops, what if your healing comes through tears? What if a thousand sleepless nights are what it takes to know You're near? What if my greatest disappointments or the aching of this life, is the revealing of a greater thirst this world can't satisfy? What if trials of this life, the rain, the storms, the hardest nights...are your mercies in disguise?*
>
> - Laura Story, *Blessings* ©
> Capitol Christian Music Group,
> Capitol CMG Publishing,
> Warner Chappell Music, Inc

DEAL WITH IT: GROUP 1

1. Which of the first four contentions unsettles you most? (Remember, rebellion is covered in the *next* section!). How easy is it to believe that these contentions might be valid? What might it mean if they are?

2. How would you describe your value system? How comfortable are you with it? To what do you attribute your values?

3. Why do you think that we retain so little of some experiences, yet can recall others with great clarity? Why is it you can vividly recall your first sexual experience...but can't remember which shirt you wore two days ago? What other "drives" lead to vivid and permanent memories in your life story? What sorts of things do you least recall? Why do you think that is?

4. How would you describe the activities and pursuits you desire most? Which would you say are *urgent*, and which are *important*? Which satisfy you most? What percentage of your waking life is spent in pursuit of your own desires, and how much is directed for the benefit of others? Are you comfortable with this? Is your allocation to these pursuits sustainable? Ever consider why you have the priorities that you presently do?

5. What was your reaction to the contention that *You Live In A Fallen World*? Does it *feel* true? Does it *seem* valid? Do you want it to be?

FURTHER READING:

John Eldredge, *Epic: The Story God Is Telling and the Role That Is Yours to Play,* Thomas Nelson, Inc., 2004. An all-round excellent read, video, and study.

Rick Warren, *The Purpose Driven Life: What on Earth Am I Here For?* Copyright 2002, Rick Warren. Also available as a Zondervan ebook. Required reading for those curious about this subject.

Jordan Peterson, *12 Rules for Life: An Antidote to Chaos.* 2018, Random House Canada. Specifically, Rule 2 and Rule 6 for this section.

CHAPTER 3 AND GROUP TWO
CONTENTIONS 5-8

WHAT YOU HAVE

5. **You have a desire to worship**
6. **You have a rebellious nature**
7. **You have gifts and abilities**
8. **You have a craving for relationships**

All of life is action and passion, and not to be involved in the actions and passions of your time is to risk having not really lived at all.

- Herodotus

YOU WERE BORN WITH SPECIAL STUFF

Bob Buford's *Halftime* and Rick Warren's *The Purpose Driven Life* make a similar point: *people who don't know their purpose try to do too much.* As Buford puts it, "No one is more in a hurry than someone who feels distracted with what he is doing now." Being 'off-purpose' causes stress, fatigue and conflict. This point can be pushed still further: until you come to terms with *what* you are and *how* you came to be here, you *cannot* know your life's purpose and intention.

In *The Purpose Driven Life*, Warren argues that *everyone's life is driven by something:*

"Some people are driven by guilt—running from regrets and hiding their shame. Some are driven by resentment and anger—they hold onto hurts and never get over them. Some are driven by materialism—a desire to acquire becomes the overarching goal of their lives. Some are driven by a need for approval—the expectations of others consumes them."

To that I will add one more: there are some who *seem* to sincerely know their purpose—though as noted earlier, it *is* possible to be sincerely wrong! Knowing your purpose gives meaning to life. And your heart surely yearns for meaning.

Do you think elephants ever wonder *"what's the point"*? Can you imagine that woodchucks do? OK...now some of you are wondering what goes on in the mind of a woodchuck. Go ahead, I'll wait...

I have observed elephants on the Serengeti. An awe-inspiring sight to be sure. From what I could tell, they didn't seem the least bit restless with the wonderment of their being...elephants. Our safari group observed them going about their normal elephant thing. The only distraction I sensed among them was a mild annoyance at being gawked at by tourists. But other than the interruption that was me, those elephants seemed perfectly content with *being* elephants. Now...they *may* have been stressed in search of food, or they *may* have been suspicious of a pride of lions lounging not so far away. But nothing about those elephants conveyed to me that they wanted to be *anything other than what they were*. My hunch is that God made them *content* with being elephants.

We humans are not blessed with such contentment. We are not so very satisfied with being...mortal. And that is what gives rise to these contentions.

Just as I claim no expertise about the mind of a woman, I'm probably no better with elephants. But to the best of my knowledge—and *as far as anyone knows*, it is only us humans who agonize over our *purpose* on the planet. Maybe someday the woodchucks will tell us different. And I think one should always be optimistic about elephants.

You *wonder* for a reason...because I made you that way. You were made for a purpose, and you are driven to find it. *You were created to pursue meaning* above all creatures that walk, fly, or crawl. *You know in your heart* that you preside on the earth and over every other creature that is on it. You *fear* other creatures--because some of them can eat you. But you don't fear that they are *greater* than you are, or that they can enslave you to serve their purpose. Only other humans will do that. I Am the reason that you view your life in this way. It is only the woman who can domesticate you ☺.

CONTENTION 5: YOU WERE BORN WITH A DESIRE TO WORSHIP

The greatest problem with communication is the illusion that it has been accomplished.

- George Bernard Shaw

There is a longing in your heart to belong to something that completes you. Something that thrills you, infuses your spirit and draws your continuous devotion. It's as though you were born with a hole in your chest, and the desire of your heart is to fill that hole with a special 'something'. To ful*fill* you (ref: Shel Silverstein: *The Missing Piece* -a great book to enjoy with bourbon). Left to your own devices you will pursue all manner of passions (gods) to satisfy this longing for fulfillment. To fill up the hole. You will worship celebrity, sex, fame and power--even "good works" to quench this longing. You might celebrate openly...or hide a monster inside of you. You might adorn yourself with a tattoo or t-shirt, celebrating the object of your affection. The evangelical term for this this *idolatry*. But no earthly pursuit can satisfy us for long, and that's just the way that it is. We can outlive our heroes, or they can outlive us. Outliving idols, after all is as old as... the Molech pictured in chapter one.

Worshiping idols will fatigue you, bankrupt you. Pursuit of this practice will wither, exhaust and consume you. That's because you were made to be filled with My spirit. I Am the source of abundant life for you. You cannot be satisfied with the worship of your choosing. You can only be completed in Me. I Am the giver of life and abundance. All else is a taker-away.

I didn't give you this desire for selfish reasons. The bible says that I Am a jealous God, but worship is a *gift* I have given you. Worship brings *you* joy. It brings *you* elation. It brings fulfillment and a sense of belonging for *you*. I don't need your worship—however sincere it may be. My receiving it is a confirmation of *your choices* in life. What you worship is a demonstration of *choice*. *Your* choice. Pretty cool, huh?

Dominican writer Albert Nolan makes the point this way:

> *"The cultural ideal of the Western industrialized world is the self-made, self-sufficient autonomous individual who stands by himself or herself, not needing anyone else...and not beholden to anyone for anything...This is the ideal that people live and work for. It is their goal in life, and they will sacrifice anything to achieve it. This is how you "get a life for yourself". This is how you discover your identity.*

> *There have been plenty of people in the past with inflated egos—kings, conquerors, and other dictators—but in the Western world today the cultivation of the ego is seen as the ideal for everyone. Individualism permeates almost everything we do. It is a basic assumption. It is like a cult. We worship the ego."*

> - Albert Nolan, Jesus Today: A
> Spirituality of Radical Freedom

> *"You can shut Him up for a fool, you can spit at Him and kill Him as a demon: you can fall at His feet and call him Lord and God. But let us not come up with any patronizing nonsense about His being a great human teacher. He has not left that open to us. He did not intend to."*

> - C. S. Lewis, *Mere Christianity*

In our consumer culture, even religion and spirituality can become a matter of addiction: joining the "right" church, touting celebrity ministers, modeling moralistic behaviors and taking mission trips to 'earn points' with God. But authentic Christianity is not about getting, attaining, performing or succeeding—all of which pander to the ego. Christianity is about letting go—letting go of the idols we clutch inside our heart-holes. Things that we don't need--though we won't know that until we focus our lens on the God who made us.

> *"God is not found in the soul by adding anything, but by a process of subtraction."*

> - Meister Eckhart 1260-1328.

(Richard Rohr's Daily Meditation from December 13, 2020 was adapted as a source for this section.)

We finish this brief contention with a reminder: In our human frame of reference, there is no such thing as "objective reality". That means it's *not possible* for you to see things "as they are". We only view and evaluate our environment through the filter—the lens we have chosen. Taking on God's filter and God's focus means purposefully letting go of our own. As Andy Stanley puts it, *the purpose of prayer is to align ourselves with God's will, not to impose our will.* Prayer and worship don't begin with asking...they begin with *recognizing.* Prayer acknowledges your reliance on the One who made you.

Worship changes things. Prayer changes things. *Prayer and worship change you and the way that you align with the world.* That is no small contention. Your heart and your mind interact during worship. Lifting up priorities in worship and in prayer build commitment and determination in your activities and your choices. Worship instills. Worship inspires. It enforces. It changes who you are and what you pursue. This is a big deal. Because God made you that way.

CONTENTION 6: YOU WERE BORN WITH A REBELLIOUS NATURE

> *In theory it is easy to convince an ignorant person; but in the affairs of real life no one offers himself to be convinced, and we hate the man who has convinced us. But Socrates advised us not to live a life which is not subjected to examination.*

> - Epictetus, Discourses, Book 1

I AM God, so let's start with this: put Me first, don't worship idols, use My name with respect and remember My sabbath. In all your affairs, respect your parents, don't hurt people, honor marriage, don't steal, don't lie and don't be envious of other people's stuff. These are the guardrails of humanity.

You are the only creature that needs operating instructions. So I gave you rules that align with the way that I made you. You call them 'commandments', which is an overly authoritative word choice in my opinion. The truth is that you *thrive* when you follow My operating instructions, and every culture on earth can understand them. You should be praising these rules, you should be grateful for them. But they are absolute, and that conflicts with your nature.

You feel tension in your neck when you think about absolutes. That's where the term "stiff-necked" comes from! But consider that *all will go well* if you put Me first, if you rest in Me and if you are

respectful of others. My instructions are *the* path to fulfillment in your life. For *your* benefit. For your understanding of who I AM—and who you are in Me.

We don't like being told what to do. And we don't generally like being directed by others. Nobody in history has ever settled down because somebody told them to '*settle down!*'. Here is an example of this:

Imagine that you've entered a lecture hall. You take a seat and size up the considerable audience around you. The speaker approaches a podium and taps the live mic with his finger. Amplified thuds reverberate through the room. *Annoying,* thinks you. The room gets quiet.

"Ladies and gentlemen", the speaker tersely begins. "*Ple-ee-ze may I have your attention!*"

He glowers at the audience, insisting on the attention of those assembled. In a moment, all eyes are focused on the speaker.

"*Now...*" he continues, in a measured tone, "I want you...to listen...*very* carefully..."

The room is silent. He has their full attention.

"I am going to be speaking from this podium for approximately the next *forty*-five minutes. While I am speaking, it is *absolutely critical* that you follow one instruction. From this moment forward, no matter what happens, do not look towards the back of the room". He admonishes his audience with a wagging finger for emphasis. *"Under no circumstances are you to turn and look at the back of the room!"*

Oh, boy. What is the *first* thing you want to do in that situation? In fact, what is the *only* thing you want to do? How long do you think you could last in such a state? How long would anyone? You can picture, in fact, the entire 'stiff-necked' room wanting to turn at once in defiance of the commanding speaker. Some people are nervously chucking...others are experiencing a mild degree of panic. *Your attention is on the back of the room!*

At first this is curiosity, right? But then it *quickly* becomes self-will. "Who are *you* to tell me what I can and cannot do? As soon as somebody tells you to *not*...you *want* to! At a minimum, you want to know *why not*? If you intend to limit me, *I* want an explanation! *You* want to be The Decider for you. The Determiner of your own fate. The Captain of Your Own Soul. And **why** do you think that is? You guessed it....

There is a reason you were created with self-will. I did that to make you an example. Your rebellious nature is an example to *Heaven* of what happens when you demand your own way. Sometimes your selfishness is funny to watch, but far more often it is painful to observe from Heaven's view. Among the most tender expressions in Christian ministry is this one: your *will must be* "broken" before you can take up My lens and follow Me. Ouch.

Now, the auditorium speaker is just an example, and this contention can be illustrated in many ways. You can't make yourself *not* think of pink elephants, after all! We are *made* to want our own way, and it often doesn't matter what "the rules" are! You are wired to submit to authority *only after* you've evaluated your options for doing it your way. That is a part of free will. It is how God made you.

Our spirit is not simply one of blatant defiance. For any number of reasons, we also don't like to 'listen'—aka follow instructions. In *12 Habits for Life*, Jordan Peterson cites the research of physician prescriptions:

> *"Imagine that a hundred people are prescribed a drug. Consider what happens next. One-third of them won't fill the prescription. Half of the remaining sixty-seven will fill it, but won't take the medication correctly. They'll miss doses. They'll quit taking it early. They might not even take it at all".*
>
> - Jordan Peterson, Habit #2: Treat Yourself Like Someone You're Responsible for Helping (cited, Annals of Internal Medicine)

A baby's first word is often "*No!*" - because that is the word babies hear most often from their parents! Ask a mom or dad with a child of that age: two-year-old humans are among the most violent species on the planet. Two-year-old's don't need to be taught how to be selfish. They kick, they hit, they scream, they bite and they take stuff from others of their kind. Until they adopt social norms (which hopefully will be drilled into them by said intrepid parents), those toddlers only know that it's "all about me!". Who would argue that honoring parents and keeping your hands to yourself isn't a good idea? And who wouldn't acknowledge that bad stuff will happen when you *don't* follow those stodgy Ten Commandments? It takes time, but eventually (hopefully), we conform to rules of mainstream behavior. Maybe some contemporary marketing whiz should re-label the Ten Commandments as "Ten Irrefutable Rules for Self-Fulfillment". Really.

Here is a challenge for the willing: If you're a praying person (and even if you're not), try asking God sometime what *He* might like to accomplish in your life. Where is *He* working, and what would put a smile on *His* face? Seems a bit extraordinary, doesn't it? But it appeals to you in a way that you probably didn't expect. And if you're a praying person, it's a *very* good idea once you think about it: What would put a smile on His face?

In the fullness of time, His answers may astonish you. You have an in-born tendency to believe that life is all about you...until one day...you realize that it isn't. And what you do on that day can determine your future. Forever.

Why is it always easier to consider what God could accomplish *through* you rather than *for Him?* Your humble author contends (once again for good measure) that it's because you *want* truth to be personal. It is natural to treat your opinions as reality. As fact. But the *fact* that you've read through these contentions thus far...means (perhaps!) that you're open to an alternate reality:

The reality that *truth* exists independently of you.

Put this book or tablet down if necessary to pull yourself together after that one.

It is hard to admit that you *can't* know truth. Instead, it is easier to admit that your *opinions can change*. Opinions can change as a result of life experience, and they can change because of what you had for dinner last night.

In Danny Kahneman's fascinating book titled *Noise,* he cites example after example of how judicial sentences are influenced by the weather, by a defendant's birthday, whether it's before lunch or after, and even by the sentences a that a judge has passed down before he finally gets to your case. Innocent…innocent…innocent…innocent---well *somebody's* got to be guilty!

After a meal, your body's digestive system jumps into high gear. Blood flow to the stomach and intestines increases. When this happens, your body decreases the supply of oxygen to the brain. This reduced supply of oxygen is what can make you feel sleepy after eating – and impairs your cognitive abilities. *You are prone to make a different decision after dinner from the decision you would have made before dinner.* Your conscious mind is just that sensitive and volatile. What you eat also influences the way you feel: when you eat foods high in sugar and carbs, your body releases more insulin. Insulin is a peptide that lowers blood sugar. If your body releases a lot, it can make your blood sugar 'crash'. You'll feel tired and less able to concentrate. How do you feel *now* about "personal truth?" Feel like asking that magistrate what he had for lunch before he announces his verdict for that speeding ticket? Talk about truth staring you in the face!

We are not objective beings…so we are not dependable arbiters of truth. That's a big one. But you *crave* truth to help you navigate your life's course—because that is the way you were designed.

If you ask…and *allow* Me to use you for the purpose for which I made you, I will. It is possible to avoid your purpose—you can choose to be inert, after all, and you can choose to actively work against Me. Your decisions are important. Your decisions not only affect your life, but the lives of those around you. Today, tomorrow and for generations yet to come. *That* reality should inspire urgency in your heart. YOU are important. Your choices and your opinions have consequences for you, your children…and for *their* children. So get over your feelings of insignificance and inadequacy. You truly are *significant*.

Knowing Me and adopting My lens is your *opportunity* to model truth and character that *truly* is yours. The fruit of good character is peace. You recognize nobility

when you see it. You recognize self-righteousness, too. When My truth is in you, others will see it. You were made to recognize the difference between nobility and selfishness. Reality works that way.

The missionary Jim Elliot put it like this: "He is no fool who gives what he cannot keep in order to gain what he cannot lose." It's common for us to think that God wants us to "give up" things in order to please Him. Nowhere does God tell us to give up things, behaviors or practices just for the sake of bowing to a selfish deity. What is called for is an acknowledgment of who God is in the daily affairs of our lives. Everything else will flow from appreciation of just that one thing. *God loves us not because we are perfect, but because we are His.*

CONTENTION 7: YOU WERE BORN WITH SPECIAL GIFTS AND ABILITIES

Everybody is a genius. But if you judge a fish by its ability to climb a tree, it will live its whole life believing that it is stupid.

- Amos Dolbear

The two highest quests in life are the desire to be loved and the desire to make a difference. To believe that happiness is the highest quest...is a shallow belief indeed.

- Clay Stephen Roberts

You have gifts that came wrapped up in who you are. Your athletic prowess (or lack thereof), your looks, your intellect, all came tucked inside the package that delivered you (literally). The spark that's inside of you (and in *every* living creature) arrived in its time and was born in its culture for a reason. This is not pre-destination. It's opportunity, baby!

The fact that you are reading this page means you've already won the lottery. You won on the day that you were born. In order to be here today, you needed:

2 parents
4 grandparents
8 great-grandparents
16 second great-grandparents
32 third great-grandparents
64 fourth great-grandparents
128 fifth great-grandparents
256 sixth great-grandparents

512 seventh great-grandparents
1,024 eighth great-grandparents
2,048 ninth great-grandparents

Your being here required the fostering DNA of 4,094 capable, participating ancestors over the last 400 years or so. And human history goes back a *lot* further than 400 years. Think about that. How many stories? How much hope? How much sacrifice, struggle and aspiration? Beyond the relational element, consider the timing, the happenstance and the destiny that all had to fall in place. Yes, your very consideration of the words on this page testifies to the jackpot that is your life. So...how far of a leap is it to consider that chance was assisted by purpose, intention...and reason?

To contend that you were created for a *reason* is not the same as saying that you were born on the earth for a *mission*. Or not necessarily. Eons of evolution equipped your human genes to get you started with a supportive set of traits. Some of your traits are common to all humans, others are somewhat customized – based on your mother and father-- and at least a *few* are unique to you compared to all humans that have *ever* existed on the planet. The snowflake thing is a similar example: lots of similarity, but no two exactly the same anywhere, ever. Our singular privilege as humans is that we are introspective about *what to do* with *who* we are, and with *what we have* to work with. We are *exclusive*. And that is quite cool.

> "There's a difference between your calling and your career. Your career is what you're paid to do; your calling is what you're made to do. A person with a calling is a person who has purpose and

meaning that will not end with the termination of a job. Those who are 'called' will go find new directions by virtue of how they were wired by God and what they were called to do."

- Howard Hendricks as quoted
in Bob Buford's *Finishing Well*

The only thing that stands between a man and what he wants to accomplish in life is often merely the will to try it and the faith to believe it is possible.

– Richard M. DeVos

Among the contentions of BIMYTW—this one may strike a nerve that runs deeper than some others. There are *reasons* you were born a bit special...though you might could be frustrated (southern phrasing) if life isn't celebrating your particular superpower at the moment. If your culture prizes swimmers and you rock the freestyle—that's well and good for you. But if your culture prizes tree climbers, that freestyle could be leaving you in the shallows. You *could* be the *best* swimmer ever born in your time, but without a platform to distinguish your specialness, that gift could go entirely unappreciated. For your whole life. Or maybe your parents couldn't afford you good lessons. Or maybe you were born in the desert.

Or maybe.

Or maybe.

Remember Archimedes: "You need both a lever and a place to stand in order to move the world". The fact that

Archimedes died in 212 BC goes to show that we've been *contending* with this predicament for a long time.

One of my favorite children's books is *A Porcupine Named Fluffy* by Helen Lester. Check it out the next time you're feeling 'misplaced'. The story gets good when a rhino named Hippo threatens to give poor Fluffy a 'rough time' (like *The Missing Piece*, it's another book best paired with bourbon, in my opinion).

But my point is this, gentle reader: perhaps you find yourself being celebrated in your time. Or maybe you're waiting to be "discovered". Perhaps you're mad at the world for not appreciating your abilities, or you've given up on your 'specialness' altogether. Why is that? Because *life's not fair*?

"Fairness" is a concept of your invention, not Mine. Fairness has always been a personal perspective. Fairness *depends* upon your *lens*.

> *Man is a deterministic device thrown into a probabilistic universe.*
> — Amos Tversky, quoted in *The Undoing Project* by Michael Lewis

Unfair, unlucky, unfortunate, inconvenient. These are opinions that we form. "Things don't upset us", the philosopher Epictetus wrote, "our judgment about them does". Events as they happen are neither fair nor unfair. They just are. Without a certain *reckoning*, though, you are left to the whims of your opinion…or someone else's opinion. Without initiative to understand truth, you are left to value truth on your own.

And that might seem like a good thing, since we don't like being told what to do ☺.

> It has been acceptable for some time in America to remain "wound identified" (that is, using one's victimhood as one's identity, one's ticket to sympathy, and one's excuse for not serving), instead of using the wound to "redeem the world," as we see in Jesus and in many people who turn their wounds into sacred wounds that liberate both themselves and others.
>
> - Richard Rohr, *Falling Upward – A Spirituality for the Two Halves of Life*

So what do 'reckoning' and 'initiative' have to do with gifts and abilities? As it turns out, everything.

In Romans, Paul wrote "*Since the creation of the world, God's invisible qualities—his eternal power and divine nature—have been clearly seen, being understood from what has been made, so that men are without excuse.*" Romans 1:20 (NIV).

This is one of the strongest contentions that Paul the apostle ever made. Paul says that you were *made* to recognize that there is a God. And unless you take initiative—unless you acknowledge and pursue a Christian value system, it is doubtful that you will *ever* understand how to deploy the special skills *you know you have. It is quite possible that your most valuable skills won't even make sense to you without the proper focus.* In the same way that you can't use a manual written in Japanese to repair a Japanese car unless you can read and understand Japanese, it is hard to "drive" the mind when you don't understand the rules of the operating system.

The appropriate value system equips and enables your mind to function in the way it was intended—*independent of the culture*—and sometimes in spite of the culture.

This is a life-changing truth.

Know why super-hero stories are so popular? Not just in America – but all around the world? Super-heroes get *celebrated*…and are sometimes *redeemed* by using their special skills.

As the story typically unfolds, a young super-hero is living the life of an oddball outcast…until fate provides the opportunity to deploy a special ability. In the pivotal moment, he is *oriented*. He has *purpose*. He has learned how to *contribute* with his gift. We admire the superhero from then on. It no longer matters what society thinks of him (though in the movies, the superhero is almost always celebrated and wins the girl's heart in the end). He is *affirmed*. He has contributed. He's *made a difference*.

Surprising the chord that this strikes in our hearts, isn't it?

There is a reason this theme is so popular.

In his enlightening book and study program titled *Epic*, John Eldredge does a terrific job making this point:

> "…Notice that every good story has the same ingredients. Love. Adventure. Danger. Heroism. Romance. Sacrifice. The Battle of Good and Evil. Unlikely heroes. Insurmountable odds. And a little fellowship that in hope beyond hope pulls through in the end.

...All the great stories pretty much follow the same story line. Things were once good, then something awful happened, and now a great battle must be fought or a journey taken. At just the right moment (which feels like the last possible moment), a hero comes and sets things right, and life is found again.

Have you ever wondered why?

Every story, great and small, shares the same essential structure because every story we tell borrows its power from a Larger Story, a Story woven into the fabric of our being...

What if all the great stories that have ever moved you, brought you joy or tears--what if they are telling you something about the true Story into which you were born, the Epic into which you have been cast? We won't begin to understand our lives, or what this so-called gospel is that Christianity speaks of, until we understand the Story in which we have found ourselves. For when you were born, you were born into an Epic that has already been under way for quite some time".

- Segmented from John Eldredge,
Epic – 2004, Nelson Books

You play tapes in your head about your obsessions and desires. Everybody does. There is an inborn craving that causes you to do this—to visualize the act of ...making a difference. Those self-soothing daydreams might be embarrassing if brought into the open. But what inspires them? Are they noble? Are they the best of you? What is *ambition*, anyway? A cycle can develop, and not necessarily a healthy one. The drive for an outlet can advance one's success...or one's shame. Songwriter Amanda Palmer writes: "If you don't deal with your demons, they go down into the cellar of your soul and lift weights." That's scary.

A variety of surveys, assessments and manuals are marketed to help you discover your strengths, your personality type and (my personal favorite) your Enneagram number. These profiles take me back to my race jockey obsession and the desire to pursue my childhood dream (chapter 1). But reality was riding a faster horse...and caught up with my ambitions. The race was futile...and time is fleeting.

James Dobson tells the story of a 50-something dentist who was complaining about the plight of his career choice. "*How dare that 22-year old decide who I would become today! What was he thinking?*" Frustration can build as life goes on. Regret can darken the skies overhead as choices are made and the path of our lives becomes narrower. What I mean, gentle reader, is that *there is an urgency to learning* who you are. The abilities you were born with are unlikely to offer as much at 75 as they might at 35. While that doesn't mean you can't fulfill destiny at an advanced age, your time to contribute can be diminished.

> *Each of us is given a pocketful of time to spend however we may. We use what we will. We waste what we will. But we can never get back a day.*
>
> *-Roger Wilcox*

Don't be too hard on yourself if you haven't been successful in your own eyes. Chance is a fascinating thing. Somebody will always be on top. If there wasn't a Warren Buffet, the market would create one. That is the nature of probability. But do you want to leave your life to chance? And how would you describe your "top"?

> *Destiny is categorically greater than potential. The apostle Peter appears to have been a pretty mediocre fisherman. The only time he caught fish, it seems, is when Jesus performed miracles! But let's say Peter had the talent to catch fish. Maybe, just maybe, if he devoted himself with the greatest passion and dedication, Peter could have become one of the top four or five fishermen on the entire Sea of Galilee. Maybe that was his potential.*

> *But even if he'd accomplished that, it wasn't his destiny. Destiny is the ordained intention God has sacredly prepared with your name on it. It is greater than potential like a gold brick is greater than a microwaveable chicken pot pie. Peter's destiny was to become a fisher of men's hearts. Even today, Peter draws us to God. That's destiny. It wasn't something Peter could manipulate, coerce or talent his way into. It's up to God, and it involves His glory, your fulfillment, and the welfare of others.*

> - The Cure, John Lynch, Bruce McNichol, Bill Thrall, copyright 2011

There are a bunch of quotations included here in Contention 7, because plenty of thoughtful people have pondered this curious condition. We'll finish with a quote from Henry David Thoreau:

> *Most men live lives of quiet desperation.*

Don't be one of those most. Mediocrity has consequences.

You know that you don't want to live among the 'most'. You know that you are special. The truth is that you are special to Me. You desire to be loved and you desire to make a difference. Because I made you that way.

CONTENTION 8: YOU CRAVE RELATIONSHIPS

Your friends determine the direction and the quality of your life.

- Andy Stanley, *Guardrails*

Community improves self-awareness. People you care about have influence in your life and can offer observations that you can't see. Allowing others to speak into our lives enables us to share vulnerabilities and worries. We are hyper-social creatures. We are creatures of interpretation, seeking other's opinions as we formulate our own. People with committed relationships lead longer, happier lives. Long-term relationships reinforce a worldview. And importantly, they provide a *consistent frame of reference* in our lives.

Our friends do indeed determine the direction and the quality of our lives. As Andy Stanley writes in *Guardrails*, we migrate towards acceptance *regardless of the quality of the group*. We are wired to seek acceptance and approval from others. Everybody wants to be loved! Once accepted, we tend to drop our guard—for the better or the worse of our direction. *Acceptance* is just that important in the way God made us.

Here are a few pearls from *Guardrails* that offer a test for the quality our relationships. Get concerned about your friends when:

- You catch yourself pretending to be someone you're not.
- You feel pressure to compromise your values.

- Something that has not previously been a temptation now is seeming to become one--because of your friends.
- Your friends are headed in a direction that you don't want to go.

People are known by their reputations—and we like to enhance ours by associating with people who *appear* to have attractive reputations. But God did an amazing thing with the capacity of the human mind: we can distinguish between *character* and *reputation*. *Character* is who *we* know *we* are. What's inside and what you're "made of." *Reputation* is who others *think* you are. The bigger the gap between your character and your reputation, the more likely it is that *someone* is being deceived. That *somebody's* lens is cloudy. The Portuguese word for this is *desconfiada*, the uneasy feeling that something isn't right. David Salyers puts it this way: "Whatever is down in your well...will eventually come up in your bucket." Oh my.

Unhealthy relationships tend to evoke the following emotions:

Guilt- I owe you
Anger – you owe me
Greed – I owe me
Jealousy – life owes me

Feel a twinge of *desconfiada* with any of this? If God wired us to crave relationships, then *every* relationship—from our parents to our lovers, is worth evaluating through our chosen lens. Another pearl from *Guardrails*: "*A person who hasn't been careful with his own life won't be careful with yours*". So whose lens are you choosing?

As I wrote earlier, this book evolved from discussions with my Northpoint Community Church men's group. While I sometimes refer to our group as a gentlemen's 'beer and bible study', the 'cheerful flow' of our discussion can raise direct and pointed questions—at each other. Our group is not for the faint of heart. While we respect each other, we do not suffer fools - and we don't cut each other slack when questioning motivation. While most of us wouldn't have chosen to be friends outside of our 'small group' environment, our commitment to 'do life together' and benefit from our varied paths has proven enormously beneficial. Over the years, each of us has suffered setbacks in life. Our current members have been meeting weekly for more than five years. We've endured crises (physical, personal, professional), we've celebrated comebacks and victories. Occasionally somebody gets angry and leaves. We've (regrettably) discussed ejecting rogue members (self-election has made that unnecessary, thank goodness) ...but the several of us who form the core of the group *keep coming back*. Our honesty and candor and openness with each other has been a blessing acquired by trust and over time. I call this 'friendship with a purpose.' Many women would be aghast at our approach to this forum (and some have told us so!). Maybe some guys might be, too. But in large part, our life experiences together have provided the fodder for this book. And I contend that is a good thing.

Evan Haskins, one of our members, once suggested we review a brutally misogynistic book by Rollo Tomassi titled *The Rational Male*. While much of this book would drop a conservative Christian's jaw, one line from it has grounded several of our conversations: *Behavior is the only reliable indicator of motivation*. The only way to evaluate "behavior" is to seek to understand each other via discussion. And that is what we do.

Crises can grow in the gaps between our character and our personality. Healthy relationships can help guard against that.

Questions are the tools of self-discovery. But where advice can be helpful, personal reflection is even better. We are far more likely to accept change and improve our situations when conclusions are reached on our own. And only when change is desired. Good counselors know this. The desire to improve is a precondition for progress. We will adopt an insight (or an epiphany!) that *we've* discovered more readily than we will ever accept advice from someone else (contention 6). "Conversation" is often thinking and processing out loud. For this to happen effectively in our lives, we cannot be bashful about the questions we ask— nor of the struggle to manage through them. A trusted relationship provides the safety and cover to expose vulnerabilities and embarrassments. Trust is enabling...*and there is no trust without risk.* God did that. Trust always costs something. God made it that way.

Unhealthy people are generally the least relationally connected to others. Victimhood has a self-bias. There is a direct correlation between listening to others and growing in self-aware maturity. That contentious word comes to mind that we always want to demand of everyone except ourselves: *accountability.* Relationships require an accountability of some sort. Even a relationship...with our Creator.

When nothing is *challenged* in you, nothing can *change* in you. Challenge evokes change. It is when we are challenged in new ways that growth happens. Isolation is the avoidance of challenge.

Here is a story that illustrates this contention:

> A minister noticed that a member of his congregation hadn't been attending Sunday services, so he made a point to visit this certain gentleman. As they settled in front of his fireplace for conversation, the gentleman seemed comfortable with his explanation: "Well, pastor, I read my bible, I pray every morning, and I take long, contemplative walks through my woods. My faith is excellent, and I have everything I need here on my own." Upon hearing this, the minister remained silent, and together they watched the fire for a while. After some time, the minister reached over, took hold of the hearth shovel, and lifted a single ember from the coals. The ember glowed brightly as it rested on the shovel, and he placed that ember on the hearth in front of the fire. As they watched together, the ember began to cool, fading from a glowing red... finally to a cold, black ash. Without saying a word, the minister smiled at the gentleman, put on his hat...and took his leave. The man stared at that ash for a long time...and he was in attendance at service the following week.

> *But that's no life for you. You learned Christ! My assumption is that you have paid careful attention*

to him, been well instructed in the truth precisely as we have it in Jesus. **Since, then, we do not have the excuse of ignorance,** *everything— and I do mean everything—connected with that old way of life has to go.*

- Ephesians 4:20–25 MSG
(emphasis added)

It was noted earlier that we move toward groups that accepts us—*regardless* of the quality of the group. Everyone wants to be chosen. It feels *good* to be chosen. But without a standard to assess what is profitable and good, we can become accustomed to almost anything. Remember contention 1?

The lens that we use to evaluate life must be cleaned with some regularity. Good friends serve as virtual lens wipers! God will allow people to poke at your weaknesses and hurts. Relationships equip us to *bear* such criticism. To prove them out, right or wrong…and adjust where necessary. Remember: a bully can never convince you that 'yo momma don't love you!

So, let's move now to the stuff of cravings.

As commonly described, there are three forms of love:

1. Agape – godly, altruistic love
2. Phlios – Brotherly love, and
3. Eros—passionate romantic love

Each of these fills a distinct need in a man's life. And of these, eros is the toughest and most challenging…as one can argue that it eclipses all three: friendship, fidelity…and sex.

I know what arousal is to a man. I invented arousal. I know how it drives you, possesses you and can overwhelm your priorities and intentions. In most of you it is rarely satiated for long. I *designed* the way that it makes your breath quicken, your blood rush and your heart pound magnificently in your chest. *I created* that. It is the essence of what makes you male. More than any of the contentions in Bob's book, this one should inspire awe as to who I really AM. *Every male on earth* was created with the drives that you have. It is how you GOT here, after all! I know that it is not good for a man to be alone. I *made* you to crave woman as a partner—and for a special companionship.

Now, this is contemporary America, so what about men craving men? Simply put, I claim no authority to address this matter as a Christian. I contend that God made us unique individuals, and that He loves us the way that we are. The free will of a man to pursue his desires (contention #3) seemingly knows no bounds. Same holds true for women, I suppose. *Behavior is the only reliable indicator of motivation!* To my way of thinking, such deep-seated motivations are best evaluated among trustworthy friends...and in contemplation with the One who created you.

Throughout history, most marriages were formed to maximize the likelihood for survival, not to maximize personal fulfillment. I didn't change that arrangement. You did.

The guilt that you heap on yourselves about sex and partnerships, and guilt of derision from others, does not come from Me. It comes from you. There is *never*

a need to destroy yourself or to doubt your worth because of who you are. And I didn't mean "what" you are---I mean *who* you are. I designed you to ask Me *what to do with who you are*. That is what *resting in Me* means.

A woman desires a man to cherish her, to protect her and provide for her. That is the nature that God gave most women. Now, *nature* and *truth* are surely *not* the same thing...and that is why women are a mystery to men! Where a man is aroused by a woman that he finds attractive, the woman has other desires: and in order to get what she wants...the woman must satisfy...the man's desires.

Guys, this is where you *know* you fit in. This is the breath-quickening heart-pounding part that you like. The part that you *know* to be true. Her *vulnerability* is the essence of your *strength*. But what entices *you* is not generally what entices *her*. At least not for long.

In his book *His Needs, Her Needs* Will Harley does a wonderful job of distinguishing between male and female needs:

Your husband is neither right or wrong, good or bad for having different needs, nor for giving them different priorities. And neither are you. They are what they are. The big mistake is where you think his needs are the same as yours, and then trying to satisfy those needs for him. Your efforts will be unappreciated because you are addressing the wrong needs.

From his day-to-day work, Harley observed that men in general most value the need for:

1. Sexual fulfillment
2. Recreational companionship
3. Physical attractiveness in himself and his spouse
4. Domestic support
5. Admiration

And generally in that order of priority. In contrast, women desire:

1. Affection
2. Conversation
3. Honesty and openness
4. Financial support
5. Family commitment

Again, generally in that order.

Either sex can have any of these needs, and value any one of them greater than the others over time. But the *nature* of men and the *nature* of women are surely distinct in these cravings. A man will profess to a woman how much he wants her...and in due time she will lay down the law about what she craves, and how to come to terms in prioritizing cravings! We were designed to be different, and to desire each other's natures, because our amazing God made us that way.

Christian marriage is:

1. a commitment of mutual submission
2. to care for each other and to meet each other's needs
3. within a pledge to rely on God in the relationship

Women have a discernment that men can't command, and men have a command that women can't approach. In a Christian marriage, you have asked God to help you, and you've pledged your intention to pursue a partnership that is pleasing in His sight. To the extent that the natures of man and woman are so different, it is hard to imagine a mutually respectful and abiding marriage that can go the distance without Him. Andy Stanley puts it this way: *"Just because you said 'I Do', doesn't mean that you can!"* To the degree that you are incapable or unwilling to meet your spouse's needs, you should realize that your spouse is not capable of the reverse! While two people "become one" in a marriage, they remain individuals. Without a similar amount of commitment to champion each other's needs, the marriage will have a rough time. That is where you either commit to prayer and submission...or head for the exists. *God will love you either way*—but the pain and the damage and the tragedy is real. Love, too, has a cost.

THE MONSTER

Guys, we know this: there is a monster inside of us that can only be tamed with attention. Berating or dismissing or humiliating the monster just frustrates it and makes it mad---and mad monsters do scary things. *The pledge that a man makes in Christian marriage is to pursue his desire for satisfaction in one woman.* That pledge is honorable, it is exclusive, and it desperate. It is how a man fulfills his deepest expression of connection with his partner. I can only imagine that God made us this way, and that helping a woman to understand 'the monster' is key to a happy marriage.

The pressure of manly desire, for companionship and admiration, has brought the downfall of many men. Good men. Godly men. And more men than have ever heard of Jesus Christ. Your *God-given* cravings can lead to satisfaction and fulfillment in your life. But pursued without *necessary* communication, boundaries and safeguards, they can bring guilt, frustration and humiliation.

Our peculiar cultural virtues haven't helped this situation much. Passion is a hard-wired thing, and it is wonderful, because God made it that way. A woman who understands this—and *communicates* her understanding, is a blessing to the fortunate man. She has her own cravings for protection and communication, and those passions are *just as real and as important* as his cravings are for the man in her life. Both are essential—as God intended them to be. But the *distress* of a woman and the *distress* of a man who either can't---or won't acknowledge and relieve the stresses in each other, has destroyed many a beautiful marriage—Christian and not.

As even the likes of Abraham Lincoln wrote to his wife Mary: "You alone can lighten this load, or render it intolerable". Maybe Abe could have used some help with come-on lines...but surely, *the hope of every husband is that his wife will desire to satisfy him*. And *the hope of every wife is that her husband will cherish and protect her*. I contend that this arrangement works best with God in the mix...because He made us to pursue this under His care. A rope of three cords is what it takes...because He made us that way.

DEAL WITH IT: GROUP 2

1. Contention 5 holds that you were born with a desire to worship. Is there something about this you don't want to accept? Or that you appreciate?

2. Contention 6: What are your thoughts about Jordan Peterson's prescription example? Is it surprising how poorly we follow instructions...or follow through?

3. Contention 7: How much of your life is an acceptance of your circumstances, and how much do you push back on and refuse to accept? What part of your reality don't you like?

4. Contention 8 makes a lot of contentions! Does the part about trust and vulnerability resonate with you? How could such sophisticated communication exist (have evolved) without Godly design?

5. Consider the elements of a Christian marriage commitment. Can you imagine *a mutually respectful* commitment for life without dependence on God?

6. If men harbor a monster, is there an equivalent inside of a woman? Why do you think God put that in there? Be careful how you approach this one—with or without the opposite sex in attendance!

FURTHER READING:

Carolyn Gregoire: *10 Psychological Studies That Will Change What You Know About Yourself*, Huffington Post 10/18/13. If you only check out one of these further readings, let this be the one. Fascinating stuff.

Eli Finkel: *The All or Nothing Marriage: How the Best Marriages Work*, 2017, Random House. An excellent reference.

Shel Silverstein: *The Missing Piece*, Evil Eye Music, 1976. If you missed it in childhood, give it a read now. A masterpiece of western philosophy. No good library is without a copy.

Andy Stanley: *Guardrails*, 2018, Northpoint Ministries, Inc. and Zondervan. Lots of constructive guidance in this book.

Helen Lester: *A Porcupine Named Fluffy*, 1986, Houghton Mifflin Harcourt Publishing Company. Acquire it along with *The Missing Piece*.

Do you know why yawning is contagious? I just did that. I thought it would be fun. 😬

CHAPTER 4 AND GROUP 3
CONTENTIONS 9-12

WHAT YOU WANT

9. **You want money, wealth and power**
10. **You are driven to satisfy your passions**
11. **You want to pursue habits that are good for you**
12. **You want to lead yourself well**

> *Esse quam videri:* to *be* rather than to *seem.*
> - Cicero, *On Friendship*

> *You can pretty much tell what God thinks of money by the kind of people he gives it to.*
> - Will Rogers

CONTENTION 9: YOU WANT MONEY, WEALTH AND POWER

This contention speaks to our self-centered temperament. We spend much of our lives in pursuit of currencies: social currency, status currency, currency currency, political influence with others, etc. We leverage our status, we posture, we preen. We take care to *appear* as we want to be seen. If we can manipulate our circumstances for personal gain, we look good! Our peers and acquaintances will think "*Wow...how did he do that?!*" Or so it seems to us. This is the nature of man. *Most of us* strive to accumulate currencies. We transact with currency to eat, to survive, to provide comfort for ourselves and perhaps our families. We compare and compete for currencies within our circles. We show off for each other with the best that we have (owned or borrowed)...and we presume far too much of our accomplishments. We take risks in *pursuing* what we desire: wealth, influence, accomplishment, being a great lover, a tough guy, a godfather. We want to be the provider, the respected elder, the expert sought out for advice. We puff ourselves up until we laugh at our comportment—at what we *believe* we are presenting to the world. I think this is a guy thing. Am I wrong? Not all the time, and not everyone goes overboard with it...but this is a genuine male *tendency.*

God *gave* us this nature of prideful self-absorption. It is a 'habit of the flesh', so to speak. And because of that, it must be intended for our benefit. He *made* us want to project confidence and dominance to the world around us.

"The highest heavens belong to the Lord, but earth he has given to mankind."

- Psalm 115:16 (NIV)

But I don't believe we were made this way just to power our egos. God designed us this way, I think, so that we could acknowledge and direct the glory of our efforts to our Creator. Who owns our successes? Do we think it's us? If so, where does that get us? If it's God...wow—I challenge you to see what happens if you live to put a smile on *His* face! We get tripped up when success is only about us.

We find ourselves feeling a pang of envy at the smarmy whiz-kid who banks $50 million on an options trade. "How on earth could *he* have managed that?" "How can that be *fair*?" (Humility is not common among the angels of our nature ☺).

So here's the point: *the more that we gain of a thing we pursue, the less we are prudent in handling it.* We become unbalanced, and other parts of our lives start to suffer. This is the truth for most guys: we tend toward foolish behavior when we have excess. Not in all cases, and not all the time, but there's no need to cite examples here, right? As a gender, we are not famous for being *responsible* with extravagance. And isn't that ironic? Maybe dangerous? Why is it that the journey—the *striving,* keeps us focused? Must there always be a dragon that needs slaying? Why is it that accomplishments don't satisfy for long? Maybe it's not that our goals need to be bigger, but that the *objective of our striving* needs refocused.

If you like slaying dragons...what would you do if you managed to slay them all? And who's gonna clean up that mess?

> *Do not meddle in the affairs of dragons, for you are crunchy and taste good with ketchup.*

> - Suzanne McMinn

Money was a clever idea (and it was *your* idea, not Mine), but from where I sit, you would be shocked to see just how fleeting that stuff really is. You pursue jobs and career paths that you don't like...in order to make more money. You squeeze out your life to the

very last drop, and ruin perfectly good relationships. You buy things and do things to show that you're worthy of admiration. But I Am the only audience that can give you applause that satisfies. That is the way you were made.

Your best efforts may not lead to wealth or fame or success. It is not a matter of trying harder. I *created* the laws of probability and chance. They are laws, and that's just how it works.

Pay attention here: I love you. I give grace to believers because they *seek* it and to sinners because they *need* it. It is who I Am. I exist in you as a longing...that you can attempt to subdue with a grand variety of distractions. I care about you and your choices. I am generous, but remember that I am also exclusive.

I created the capability for every feeling and emotion that you have. But as you surely know, your cravings are not always in your best interest. What fills your mind is not fully within your control. That is why I must be the audience you seek.

Living beneath your means is a blessing. The tithing thing is real. It will change your life. You can live more fulfilled on 90 percent of your earnings than you ever will on 100 percent. Malachi wrote it down: *Do this and see if I don't throw open the gates of heaven and pour out so much blessing that there will not be room enough to store it.* (Malachi 3:10 NIV)

This is again why the lens we choose is so important. Because we cannot be successful in the life that God designed for us to live...if we are unaware of the character traits He put inside us.

As Alastair Begg wrote: *"When you trust in Me, no rise or fall of the markets can interfere with your salvation. No breaking banks, no failures or bankruptcies can touch that. No change of circumstance can rob you. I love you, and nothing can affect that. You are not a poor creature cast down by what happens to us in this poor, fleeting state of time."*

Christian counselor Kevin Daly likes to say that "the purpose of the bible is not just to inform, but to *transform*". What follows is the singular example in this book where a full chapter of the bible is presented for your contemplation. Each of the twelve contentions in this book are prepared from a human perspective, but as was noted earlier, our lives are not just "about us". I've written about 'commandments' and I've written about 'will'. All from the standpoint of human consideration. For reference and contrast, Jeremiah 7 describes what happens when we follow...or choose to *not* follow, God's intentions. The full chapter is presented here for comprehensive context. It amplifies the Malachi verse. As an ancient admonishment, Jeremiah warns against the pursuit of "false religion". It is wisdom for the ages, and absolutely worth the read.

JEREMIAH 7 (NIV): FALSE RELIGION WORTHLESS

This is the word that came to Jeremiah from the LORD: "Stand at the gate of the LORD's house and there proclaim this message:

Hear the word of the LORD, all you people of Judah who come through these gates to worship the LORD. This is what the LORD Almighty, the God of Israel, says: Reform your ways and your actions, and I will let you live in this place. Do not trust in deceptive words and say, 'This is the temple of the LORD, the temple of the LORD, the temple of the LORD!' If you really change your ways and your actions and deal with each other justly, if you do not oppress the foreigner, the fatherless or the widow and do not shed innocent blood in this place, and if you do not follow other gods to your own harm, then I will let you live in this place, in the land I gave your ancestors for ever and ever. But look, you are trusting in deceptive words that are worthless".

"Will you steal and murder, commit adultery and perjury, burn incense to Baal and follow other gods you have not known, and then come and stand before me in this house, which bears my Name, and say, "We are safe"—safe to do all these detestable things? Has this house, which bears my Name, become a den of robbers to you? But I have been watching"! declares the LORD.

"Go now to the place in Shiloh where I first made a dwelling for my Name, and see what I did to it because of the wickedness of my people Israel. While you were doing all these things", declares the LORD, "I spoke to you again and again, but you did not listen; I called you, but you did not answer. Therefore, what I did to Shiloh I will now do to the house that bears my Name, the temple you trust in, the place I gave to you and your ancestors. I will thrust you from my presence, just as I did all your fellow Israelites, the people of Ephraim.

So do not pray for this people nor offer any plea or petition for them; do not plead with me, for I will not listen to you. Do you not see what they are doing in the towns of Judah and in the streets of Jerusalem? The children gather wood, the fathers light the fire, and the women knead the dough and make cakes to offer to the Queen of Heaven. They pour out drink offerings to other gods to arouse my anger. But am I the one they are provoking"? declares the LORD. "Are they not rather harming themselves, to their own shame"?

Therefore this is what the Sovereign LORD says: "My anger and my wrath will be poured out on this place—on man and beast, on the trees of the field and on the crops of your land—and it will burn and not be quenched".

This is what the LORD Almighty, the God of Israel, says: "Go ahead, add your burnt offerings to your other sacrifices and eat the meat yourselves! For when I brought your ancestors out of Egypt and spoke to them, I did not just give them commands about burnt offerings and sacrifices, but I gave them this command: **Obey me, and I will be your God and you will be my people. Walk in obedience to all I command you, that it may go well with you. But they did not listen or pay attention; instead, they followed the stubborn inclinations of their evil hearts.** They went backward and not forward. From the time your ancestors left Egypt until now, day after day, again and again I sent you my servants the prophets. But they did not listen to me or pay attention. They were stiff-necked and did more evil than their ancestors.

When you tell them all this, they will not listen to you; when you call to them, they will not answer. Therefore say to them, 'This is the nation that has not obeyed the LORD its God or responded to correction. Truth has perished; it has vanished from their lips'".

Cut off your hair and throw it away; take up a lament on the barren heights, for the LORD has rejected and abandoned this generation that is under his wrath.

The Valley of Slaughter

"The people of Judah have done evil in my eyes", declares the LORD. "They have set up their detestable idols in the house that bears my Name and have defiled it. They have built the high places of Topheth in the Valley of Ben Hinnom to burn their sons and daughters in the fire—something

I did not command, nor did it enter my mind. So beware, the days are coming", declares the LORD, "when people will no longer call it Topheth or the Valley of Ben Hinnom, but the Valley of Slaughter, for they will bury the dead in Topheth until there is no more room. Then the carcasses of this people will become food for the birds and the wild animals, and there will be no one to frighten them away. I will bring an end to the sounds of joy and gladness and to the voices of bride and bridegroom in the towns of Judah and the streets of Jerusalem, for the land will become desolate".

- Jeremiah 7. Bold emphasis added.

Pretty bleak! This passage is surely counted among the "fire and brimstone" chapters of the Old Testament, but it is delivered with a commitment for restoration and protection! He is ALWAYS waiting for us. Everything I have experienced in my life has shown me that God *wants* to bless us, because He intended for us—He designed us—to be blessed. He is waiting for our best moment.

Some who've studied history have dismissed Christianity because the temple of Jerusalem was destroyed and brought to ruin. What these folks fail to understand is that God resides first in the *hearts of those drawn to acknowledge Him.* But no heart--let alone a humble home, a mansion or a yacht should expect the indwelling of the Spirit without having first experienced reconciliation and respect.

God made you to crave money, wealth and power. Use your lens to recognize and pay attention to what you do with these cravings. Use them to live your best life.

CONTENTION 10: YOU ARE DRIVEN TO SATISFY YOUR PASSIONS. IF YOU CANNOT FIND ADMIRABLE MEANS TO DO SO, YOU WILL PURSUE LESS THAN ADMIRABLE MEANS TO DO SO

Only consider at what price you will sell your own will; if for no other reason, at least for this, that you will sell it not for a small sum. Now if virtue promises good fortune and tranquility and happiness, certainly also the progress toward virtue is a progress toward each of these things. What is the product of virtue? Tranquility.

- Epictetus (AD 60-138)
Discourses, Book 1

Life is the sum of your choices.
- Albert Camus

This one might make you squirm in your chair a little, but we're going to tackle it anyway. There are direct and candid statements in the paragraphs that follow, and I leave it for you to consider if and whether these assertions characterize where you are. If you are young, this section may seem particularly strong. If you are older, these passages will be less affronting - and more familiar.

When desires are suppressed, you will pursue increasingly desperate means by which to maintain your distraction of choice.

Go back and read that again.

You will stuff those obsessions deep inside, soldier on, and conform to the expectations of your relationships and your culture. But you can do this for only so long.

I contend that men strive for honor in their lives. We are made that way. This is our 'means' to the 'end' for the admiration that was covered in Contention 8. Admiration is noble. Nobility is a virtue.

An analogy for this: It is surprising how much garbage can be compressed inside of the humble trash compactor. Not a garbage *disposal* that grinds stuff up and washes it down the drain (though that device is also a wonder of modern invention), but the modest machine that mashes stuff and creates the capacity to fit more. You just close the drawer, hit the button, and keep *stuffing* and *mashing* and *stuffing* and *mashing*, pushing stuff down further and further. It's quite handy.

It turns out that you can do this with frustrations in your life. *Years* can go by without ever emptying the receptacle. Just swallow and stuff. Swallow. And stuff. Pushing. And mashing. Until one day…with no warning whatsofrickinever…you drop in a morsel, you mash down the button. You swallow---and

KA-BLAMO!

The long-suffering machine that has soldiered on for years suddenly, finally explodes - spewing trash and gunk *all over* the place. The machine took in all that it could. It bore the burden and confined the pressure until exceeding its capacity and then some. But what ultimately happened is what inevitably happens when you don't empty the machine like you're supposed to. It bears what it can for as long as it can…and then it breaks.

In the aftermath of the explosion, amid the detritus and waste, is what Kevin Daly once told me is *the freedom that comes from release*. The trash is no longer under pressure in the box. You may be covered in mess---you and anyone around you. The machine is broken. You are broken. You won't ever get that stuff back inside the box again. *And you don't want to!* The only matter at hand now is what got broken in the disaster and …how you will address the mess that has occurred. The event itself can be a spectacular release of pressure. And hopefully the event itself put no one else in harm's way (unlikely). Before that moment, there was desperation inside—whether you (the vessel) could feel it or not. You could have been ruthless, you could have been calm, but something failed and triggered the inevitable explosion. You were soldiering on insofar as the vessel was making it possible. For as long as you could hold it in. Our drives can carry us to the very heights of heaven, or they can render us feeling shameful, dirty and broken.

By now, I hope you realize why this analogy is a good one. Because the God of heaven designed you to be this way. The fact that you can relate to this analogy doesn't make it good or bad. But it does make it relevant. In all that you are holding, gentle reader, find a way—*insist* on a way, to occasionally empty the compactor.

By now, you should also recognize that this contention is not just about sex, although sex is an easy example to employ. Men have obsessions. We just do. I don't contend to be an authority about the drives that guys have. But I've been a guy for 62 years now, so give me credit for that. It's a big world out there. While drives and obsessions come in different forms—and become unfulfilled for different reasons, those obsessions can also be...distractions.

There is a big difference between "can't" and "won't". I invite you to ponder how to distinguish between the two. I believe that's where empathy and acceptance lie. Godly men and godly women get into marital difficulty all the time. It is a tragedy. This is a book for men, so read these words: Heaven *knows* that men can be boneheads, with or without God in our lives. But even Christian marriages fail because of this tragedy. If you are married...and brave...I invite you to share this chapter with your spouse. Not that the idea hasn't occurred to you already! ☺

Desperation is humiliating, and humiliation is the opposite of admiration. Can I get an amen?

> *A woman needs a man to help her plan. A man needs a woman to focus his passions.*

> - Clay Stephen Roberts

There will be moments in life that feel like a test. Like you're being evaluated ahead of the next move. That is not paranoia. It's your conscience. I did that. Conscience is a reminder that I made rules. "He has set eternity in the human heart" (Ecclesiastes 4 NIV). That's Me. You have to navigate your choices - and live with them.

Asking Me to take away your free will to decide is *not* an option. That's why you struggle. It's one way for you to know that you need Me. If I took away the

areas where you struggle because you asked Me to, you would soon conclude that you don't need Me anymore. I am not here to meet your needs and to justify your every prayer request. That would make *you* God.

I've heard a billion requests to quell desire so that a man might stay faithful to his wife, his path and his dreams. To smash all other lenses. To take away free will. Free will is your blessing to bear.

I Am with you, and you need My presence more than you need answered prayer. A lens you have chosen doesn't make you a Christian any more than the bible created Christianity. You must pursue what is not natural to you—but is inspired. It is the *fulfilment* and *tranquility* (read: peace) you will come to experience that will persuade you that I Am The Way.

> I asked God to take away my habit.
> God said "No. It is not for me to take away, but for you to give it up."
> I asked God to make my friend's handicapped child whole.
> God said "No. His spirit is whole, his body is only temporary."
> I asked God to grant me patience.
> God said "No. Patience is a byproduct of tribulations; it isn't granted, it is learned.
> I asked God to give me happiness.
> God said "No. I give you blessings; happiness is up to you."
> I asked God to spare me pain.

God said "No. Suffering draws you apart from worldly cares and brings you closer to Me."
I asked God to make my spirit grow.
God said "No. You must grow on your own, but I will prune you to make you fruitful".
I asked God for all things, that I might enjoy life.
God said "No. I will give you life, so that you may enjoy all things".
I asked God to help me love others as much as He loves me.
God said "Ahhh, finally you have the idea!"

- Carolyn Bazik, reprinted
with permission from *Zenska Jednota*, February 2021

If you are hungry, you will steal to eat. If your children are hungry, you might kill if you had to just to feed them. The urgency of the present will always command your attention. If your urgent needs are unfulfilled, you will pursue urgent means by which to quell them. Otherwise, the craving doesn't go away. Not fun, not fair, not comfortable, not easy, but always and everywhere true. We must struggle to communicate our needs and satisfy our desires--commonly in relationship with others.

Wisdom is proved right by all her children.

- Luke 7:35 (NIV)

Like the moon, you borrow your light. God will love you regardless of your choices (your choices as well as choices foisted on you by others), but there are always consequences for the choices we make. This book contends that you should navigate choice and consequence within the construct God has provided. Sometimes free will stinks—but nothing like the detritus of a trash compactor. The mess of consequence can be ugly. "Repentance" means kicking that mess to the curb.

As Oswald Chambers writes in *My Utmost For His Highest* (February 8): Sanctification means intense concentration on God's point of view..." *Lord, make me as holy as You can make a sinner saved by grace*". The purpose of prayer is that we get hold of God, not hold of the answers we're seeking.

Bold stuff, I know. Keep going. Two contentions left.

CONTENTION 11: YOU WANT TO PURSUE HABITS THAT ARE GOOD FOR YOU, BUT THERE IS ONLY SO MUCH DISCIPLINE TO GO AROUND

The battle line between good and evil runs through the heart of every man.

- Alexander Solzhenitsyn

This one becomes apparent in the fullness of time. Some guys only learn this when struck with reality. Struck. In the head. With a chair. We aspire to be rational in the same way that some aspire to holiness.

What resonates in us is different across men and can change through the course of our lives. A broad range of activities and environments can stir our souls.

Perhaps you find your element for experiencing peace—your 'happy place', in one or more of the following:

- Naturalist: finding peace in the out of doors
- Sensate: finding peace with the senses
- Traditionalist: finding peace through tradition and ritual
- Ascetic: finding peace through solitude and simplicity
- Caregiver: finding peace by loving others
- Activist: finding peace through confrontation
- Enthusiast: finding peace with mystery, celebration and adventure
- Contemplative: finding peace through adoration
- Intellectual: finding peace with mental applications and pursuits

- Adapted from the *Northpoint Men* presentation *"Hearing From God"*

Outside of our 'native' comforts, we can quickly become challenged and unbalanced. Within our comfort zone, we right our perspective and level our approach to the world. It is the difference between "guard up" and "guard down".

Tim Keller wrote some good words on this subject in the February 13 passage of *The Songs of Jesus*:

> *David's enemies are (were) opposed to his philosophy of life. His conviction was that "a man must live by the help of God, and not by his wits," a view of life his enemies despised as naïve. David admits that without God, the life of integrity would be no match for the self-interested, treacherous power politics of the world.*

A few sentences on, Keller's prayer for the day concludes with this:

> *Give me the desire and integrity to live like this. And because this will make me vulnerable, protect me from those who would take the opportunity to harm me. Amen.*

From another angle: as he's apt to do, Oswald Chambers takes tough shots at man's approach. The quotes that follow may be more readily accepted by guys who already count themselves as Christians. But this is contention #11 of 12... so to the non-Christ-following readers, the evidence has already been piled pretty high for you...

We do not consciously disobey God, we simply do not heed Him. God has given us His commands: there they are, but we do not pay any attention to them, not because of willful disobedience, but because we do not love and respect Him.

We show how little we love God by preferring to listen to his servants only. We like to listen to personal testimonies, but we do not desire that God himself should speak to us.

The destiny of my spiritual life is such identification with Jesus Christ that I always hear God, and I know that God always hears me ... If I have not cultivated this devotion of hearing, I can only hear God's voice at certain times; at other times I am taken up with things— things which I say I must do, and I become deaf to Him.

- Quoted from *My Utmost for His Highest*, February 12 and 13

Chambers' quotes are assertive, direct and unsettling. Why are they relevant here? Because they speak to a common condition for us: we like to approach life on *our own terms*. *What* we want, *when* we want it and *as much as* we want. It is 'natural' that we prefer this. But recall the introductory chapter to this book: we *rarely* get to call the shots when it comes to big events in our lives. We are more re-actors than actors. More the choose-es than the choosers. So unless you have a bearing that begins with a source more powerful, more stable and more objective than you are...well, your story and your condition are apt to disappoint. Our habits lead to decisions, and decisions (like friends) determine the direction and the quality of our lives. *Knowing* the right things to do and *doing* them consistently is not natural to most men without 1) a consistent point of reference, and 2) reinforcement.

> *Men don't require so much to be informed as they need to be reminded.*
> - Samuel Johnson

The field of behavioral economics contends that man aspires to be rational. We *aspire* to be rational, but we are not rationally motivated beings. We are creatures of action, inspired by *emotional* motivations. Psychologists call this the "self-serving" bias. We operate with varied degrees of illusion when it comes to our abilities and confidence. A psalmist writes that we "can't see our own eyeballs", but we can surely "find the speck in our neighbor's eye." We find excuses for our own shortcomings—even when we are unhappy with our habits. Most guys aspire to a tight six-pack...but kegs are far more common. Who has the time for that, right?

Healthy habits are not common to guys unless they are approached with tangible rewards. Without a desirable goal or anticipated benefit, you will drift and become less diligent with 'aspirational' habits. And even with discipline, you require reinforcement, encouragement and support. Good habits require effort, because the current of life follows 'the path of least resistance'. Unless you are struggling against comfort to higher things, 'life' will tend to 'happen' (recall Shakespeare quote in the introduction), and you will spend your life 'wallowing in the shallows'. *Obedience, vision* and *discipline* are not comforting words. Be we know that they are admirable words.

"*Failure is easy to understand,*" says Jordan Peterson:

"*No explanation for its existence is required. In the same manner: fear, hatred, addiction, promiscuity, betrayal and deception require no explanation. It's not the existence of vice or the indulgence in it that requires explanation. Vice is easy—and failure is easy, too. It is <u>success</u> that is the mystery! Virtue—that's what's inexplicable! To fail, you merely have to cultivate a few bad habits. You just have to bide your time. And once a person has spent enough time cultivating bad habits and biding their time, they are much diminished. Much of what they could have become has dissipated, and what is lesser has become real.*"

- Adapted from *12 Rules for Life: An Antidote to Chaos* 2018, Random House Canada.

A little sleep, a little slumber a little folding of the hands to rest—and poverty will come on you like a thief and scarcity like an armed man.
- Proverbs 24:33–34 NIV

Every area of life that is important requires a push upstream. You need community and affirmation. Rarely will this happen without intention and support (remember - there is only one Warren Buffet!). You

need other people who are pursuing Me in the same way that you are—to speak into your life so that you can support each other in your struggles. I made you that way. I made you to struggle with intention. It is essential to your privilege of choice. This brings your community closer to Me.

ABOUT FAIRNESS

With all of this "aspiring" and "struggle" and "choice"...I suppose it's high time that we broach the concept of "fairness."

"Fairness," so far as we know, is a uniquely human sensibility. It sets us apart from the "survival of the fittest" regime to which the rest of life is destined. Why do we struggle with what is 'fair' or 'equitable'? Across cultures and times, the human concept of 'fairness' appears to be ever-present. *Who decides* what's 'fair'? Well, *we* do...errr...*you* do! Whether or not we are born with a sense of equity, your author does not know. But regardless of where this "sense" comes from, one notices it first in toddlers. Ever watch toddlers play? As they interact, a fascinating interplay unfolds. Who holds the ball? Who takes a turn? The looks that they give each other are classic interplay, but "Mine!" as a possessive term certainly seems more common than "you first" in toddler-speak! Perhaps empathy becomes possible as young minds mature (really?) and we seek the comradery of others. But certainly 'fairness' is a skewed concept, as we measure it in proportion to *ourselves* rather than by what others deserve in comparison to us.

And again, the reminder: *you were made this way.* Complex, but true.

So as we set our expectations--with ourselves as ultimate arbiters, I invite you to consider how important it is that the *rules* of your judgements be tested. Does your world really "revolve around you?"

Following are a few quotes and thoughts from Richard Rohr's *Falling Upward* and his *Center for Action and Contemplation*:

- Integrity has largely to do with purifying our intentions and a growing honesty about our actual motives. It is hard work. Most often we don't pay attention to that inner task until we suffer some kind of fall or failure. Life, if we are honest about it, is made up of many fallings and failings, amid our hopeful growing and achieving.

- You cannot avoid sin or mistakes anyway (Romans 5:12) and trying too fervently often creates even worse problems. Jesus loved to tell stories like the prodigal son, in which one character does his life totally right...and is in fact wrong—and the other who does life totally wrong and ends up God's beloved! Now deal with that!

- Jesus also tells us there are two groups who are very good at trying to avoid or deny this humiliating surprise: those who are very *rich* and those who are very *religious*. These two groups have special plans for themselves, as they try to totally steer their own ships with well-chosen itineraries.

- Those who are too carefully engineering their own superiority systems will usually not allow for failure... and sometimes nonreligious people are more open...to a change in strategy than are religious folks who have their own private salvation project all worked out. Your willpower and the pursuit of moral perfection can't be engineered by yourself. This is probably why Jesus praised faith and trust even more than love!

- The "not-Saul" route: Traditional preachers tend to compel the Christian faithful to "believe" or "trust" or "hold on". They are not encouraging you to just believe silly or irrational things. They are beseeching you to hold on until you can go on the further journey for yourself, and they are telling you that the whole spiritual journey is, in fact, for real—which you cannot possibly yet know. There is nothing wrong with beseeching people to believe. Just be realistic about what you are expecting from those moved to give God a try.

Adapted from Falling Upward: A Spirituality for the Two Halves of Life, 2012, Jossey-Bass, Wiley

Evaluating 'fairness' leads one to consider *what* is fair, and *who* determines fairness to begin with. You are self-aware in ways that no other creature on the earth is self-aware. *We* choose and *we* influence our reality in ways that no other of Earth's creatures can even approach (so far as we know!). But in making our choices, we are also prone to be *wrongheaded* in ways that no other creature can approach (so far as we know!). Capable of extraordinary gestures, we are, while at the same time despicable behavior (I know, this has been repeated several times—but it's important). Our models for knowledge, leadership and example have enormous and weighty implications. For us. And for everything else in our environments. "Fairness", after all, is an *opinion*.

Someone capable of causing you to believe absurdities is capable also of causing you to commit atrocities.

- Voltaire

Your willpower will never be strong enough to police your desires. Your mind pursues unharnessed thoughts that are subject to the whims of your environment, your relationships...and your digestive system. You need a lens that provides consistency and absolutes for your life to overcome the desires of your nature. That is where I come in.

Every one of us is but a single decision away from altering the course of our lives. Behavioral Science offers some valuable insights here. From an article titled *The Best Headspace for Making Decisions*:

> *Your gut, to the extent that it reflects your feelings, might be steering you wrong. Take anger, one of the emotions...psychologists understand best. Where fear breeds uncertainty, anger instills confidence. Angry people are more likely to put the blame on individuals, rather than "society," or fate. Anger makes people more likely to take risks and to minimize how dangerous those risks will be. Other researchers have shown that angry people rely more on stereotypes and are more eager to act. It's an activating emotion: In lab studies, people shown angry faces crave a reward more intensely.*
>
> *This trigger-happy impulse is evolutionarily adaptive, Lerner said. "We evolved in*

hunter-gatherer times," …"If someone steals your meat, you don't think 'Should I go after him?' No! You strike back quickly."

For a 2003 study, Lerner had a group of U.S. citizens read either a news story about anthrax mail-threats, which was meant to make them feel afraid, or one about celebrations of the 9/11 attacks by some people in Middle Eastern nations, which was meant to elicit anger. Those who were made to feel angry saw the world as less risky, and they also supported harsher measures against suspected terrorists.

- From *The Best Headspace for Making Decisions*, Olga Khazan, *The Atlantic Monthly*, September 2016)

There are good reasons for *reacting* instead of *responding* sometimes—don't let that dude take your meat! After a dramatic interaction—and sometimes within it, you are orienting and planning your next move. You assess the interplay around you and calculate an approach to your environment. Your mind is doing fantastic calculations—emotions included! Neurons are firing and the lens that you have chosen will set the focus for what happens next.

The purpose of this contention is to demonstrate that your mind has a "go-to" box for making decisions. Discipline must be an *opportunity* rather than an *obligation* in order for it not to exhaust you. In times of stress and pressure, you rely on that box for orienting rational behavior. Sometimes decisions are matter-of-fact…and sometimes they require imagination. Your rational mind and your imagination are both amazingly complex. And God put them in the same box. Sometimes you get to control what is happening in the box...and sometimes imagination throws a party in there!

Wouldn't it be useful to understand why wild, outlandish thoughts cross your mind sometimes? Why the most craven and nightmarish of thoughts can hijack your head and show you movies? Dr. Ellen Hendriksen explains it this way:

> Psychologists use the term thought-action fusion to describe the erroneous idea that thinking about something is equivalent to actually doing that thing. A variation on thought-action fusion is a mistaken belief that your weirdest thoughts are a true indicator of who you are and what you are likely to do.
>
> For example, an individual who believes in thought-action fusion might be waiting for a train and see an elderly woman waiting a few steps away on the platform. The thought "I could push that old lady on the tracks right now," might cross his mind.
>
> Most would then think, "That was random; what a strange thing to think. I'm sure not going to do that," and contentedly resume texting, reading subway ads, or staring into space.
>
> Our friend who believes that thought equals action, however, thinks that this thought means, deep down, he really wants to, or will,

send our unsuspecting granny to her demise.
He thinks, "What a horrible thing to think!
I must be losing my mind! I need to get out
of here before I kill her!" He scuttles away,
ashamed, confused, and very distressed,
convinced that having the thought is as bad
as doing the deed.

- Adapted from "Does Thinking
Wild Thoughts Mean I'm
Losing My Mind?", Ellen
Hendriksen, Ph. D., originally
published on HuffPost, 2014

Who *hasn't* had wild thoughts like that? Without a powerful lens to enforce your value system when "there is not enough discipline to go around", chaos happens.

Here are some thoughts from essayist and author David Brooks on this subject, quoted from his outstanding book *The Road to Character*:

I've discovered that without a rigorous focus
on the Adam II side of our nature, it is easy
to slip into a self-satisfied moral mediocrity.
You grade yourself on a forgiving curve. You
follow your desires wherever they lead you,
and you approve of yourself so long as you
are not obviously hurting anyone else. You
figure that if the people around you seem to
like you, you must be good enough. In the
process, you end up turning yourself into
something a little less impressive than you
had originally hoped.

Further in this book, Brooks refers to enlightened thinkers like Dante, Hume, Burke, and Berlin. He writes:

> *All of these thinkers take a limited view of our individual powers of reason. They are suspicious of abstract thinking and pride. They emphasize the limitations of our individual natures…There are bugs in our souls that lead us toward selfishness and pride, that tempt us to put lower loves over higher loves.*

As noted earlier, big-time thinking personalities have pondered this hapless condition for a long time! It is humbling to consider how little of our lives we control! One more Brooks quote (and not only because it's funny):

> *Montaigne came to realize how hard it was to control one's own mind, or even one's body. He despaired over even his own penis, "which intrudes so tiresomely when we do not require it and fails us so annoyingly when we need it most."*

Now *there's* a compelling analogy, no?

I Am the decider of what is good and what is evil. Your mind and your will are only as capable as the lens that you have chosen to guide your heart—to help manage what's going on inside "the box." You weren't designed to "have enough discipline to go around" without Me. Because I made you that way.

CONTENTION 12: YOU WANT TO LEAD YOURSELF WELL, BUT YOU CAN'T

The more unique you think your recovery needs are, the less you can be helped.

- Josh Jarvis, recovery specialist and arborist

Should you follow your heart? Well, it depends on what's in there!"

- Andy Stanley

It was almost too easy to dramatize this weird trick of the mind. People could be anchored with information that was totally irrelevant to the problem they were being asked to solve. For instance, Danny and Amos asked their subjects to spin a wheel of fortune with slots on it that were numbered 0 through 100. Then they asked the subjects to estimate the percentage of African countries in the United Nations. The people who spun a higher number on the wheel tended to guess that a higher percentage of the United Nations consisted of African countries than did those for whom the needle had landed on a lower number. What was going on here... was it a shortcut that people used, in effect, to answer to their own satisfaction a question to which they could not divine the true answer?

- Michael Lewis, *The Undoing Project*, 2017, W.W. Norton & Co.

While Socrates contended that 'an unexamined life is not worth living', he did not prompt us to do so of our own accord. We're not good at being objective about the stuff that is inside of us. David didn't see his error until Nathan pointed it out. Peter didn't see his arrogance until Paul pointed it out. It is a hard thing to ponder your own imperfections.

You need help to recognize what you either cannot or will not see inside yourself. Anybody can tell you that you're a bonehead for some reason or another. And sometimes that chair to the head is what you need!

But it is arguably better (and surely less bruising!) to have people in your life who you respect--and who are willing to point out shortcomings with kindness. Constructively. For your benefit. This is *examination*. And it is arguably better to have a value system in your life that enables you size up performance for divine improvement. Evangelists call this *sanctification*.

Among the probing questions that Bob Buford asks in *Halftime* is this one: "*Where do I look for inspiration, mentors and working models?*" (p.72). We are influenced by the words and the examples that we encounter. Words have meaning, and "ignorance of the law is no excuse".

Economist Richard Thaler's books are interesting to read, because he's a sharp-writing self-acknowledged smartass. But he's also a Nobel prize-winning economist, renowned for recognizing patterns in human behavior. In his best-selling book *Nudge*, Thaler contends that humans are easily influenced by other humans. We can be prompted to behave in conforming ways...because as individuals we *like* to conform. We like to think that we are making our own decisions (don't tell me what to do!), but we aspire even more to be *accepted*. "It's actually kind of fun to watch", says Thaler. "You think people are paying attention to you. That all of your attentions matter. Actually, they don't." Our vulnerability is what drives our appetite for conformity. So who you choose to 'conform' with matters!

When you take on a lens, you see things from the lens' perspective. A good lens brings the proper things into focus. If the lens is true, harmful distortions are eliminated. And the longer you take on a lens, and use it, you will determine for yourself if/whether that lens gives you a true focus on reality. Faith is like that.

You want to be the master of your destiny—to use your own spyglass, because there's a little of Me in you.

The lens that you choose needs to be cleaned regularly to stay sharp and in focus. The purpose of a church, a fellowship or small group is to reinforce your view and maintain focus. All of these groups are comprised of people. People on different paths, people with different intellects. But their common pursuit of Christian faith usually means that they are seeking God's exclusive lens. A healthy church keeps a goodly supply of lens wipes on hand! As I wrote earlier, we are all people, but the people you choose to surround yourself with…well, you know…

I Am truth and I Am life. Nobody comes to salvation except through Me. Because I Said So.

I am pulling for you. I love you. You were not made to live in the world where you are. You live in a fallen world, you were born with no moral compass, and

you are driven to worship with imperfect vision. What could possibly go wrong?!

You have the free will to make decisions. My knowledge of what is going to happen in your choosing doesn't make Me responsible for your choices. Some like to think that life is all predestination. That philosophy lets you off the hook! As much as you might want it differently, you are responsible for the choices that you make. That's why I've given you so much evidence about to who I Am (Romans 1). I know that you are capable of choosing Me. And by now, you know why.

As the twelfth and final of these contentions, which I hope have inspired you to epiphany (!!!), this is a good one with which to bring this study to a close. In your author's experience, Contention 12 is not hard to accept...and may well be the one that sustains you through life (one epiphany can be good for a lifetime!). I believe that that *most folks hunger for the same intentionality that you do.* We all want to be recipients of good advice. We all aspire to wisdom--not *opinion,* but *wisdom.* We know how to distinguish between *advice* and *example.* As guys, we're usually quick to offer advice--it's our nature to want to fix what we think needs fixing. But the people we choose to surround ourselves with for support and advice will ultimately serve as our interpreters. To a great degree, Contention 12 is a tip-of-the-hat to my Northpoint men's group—and similar platforms that help "iron sharpen iron". I believe that God provides such people, churches and platforms when we ask Him to. *If you ask God to show you who He is, He will.*

As you've made it this far, I offer for your consideration one last passage from good ol' Oswald. Oswald Chamber's words are sometimes terse—sometimes sharp...and in following excerpt he is both—and he accomplishes a profound point of context with which to close this study.

"...*My claim to my right to myself entered the world through one man, and that another man took on Him the sin of the human race and put it away—is an interestingly profound revelation.* **The disposition of sin is not immorality and wrong-doing, but the disposition of self-realization—I am my own god.** *This disposition may work out in decorous morality or indecorous immorality, but it has the one basis,* **my claim to my right to myself.**

Sin is a thing I am born with and I cannot touch it; God touches sin in Redemption." "God nowhere holds a man responsible for having the heredity of sin. The condemnation is not that I was born with a heredity of sin, but if when I realize Jesus Christ came to deliver me from it, I refuse to let Him do so, from that moment I get the seal of damnation. "And this is the judgement" (the critical moment), "that the light is come into the world, and men loved the darkness rather than the light."

- *My Utmost for His Highest, October 5,*
"*The Bias of Degeneration", emphasis added*

Thanks for the read. I hope by now that the practical evidence for the way God made you is piled high and seems mighty compelling. You were *made* for God's love. He offers nothing less than your best life. And then the party begins.

Don't miss the party.

No one is asked to commit intellectual suicide in order to become a Christian. There is enough rational evidence to convince any reasonable person that Jesus Christ is who He said He is.

- Josh McDowell

Your legacy is determined by your final chapter, not your finest chapter.

- Andy Stanley

DEAL WITH IT: GROUP 3

1. We all know what we *want* at the moment. You might describe your 'wants' one way now...and differently tomorrow. 'Want' is a term that needs attribution: "Want" for what? To help me sleep? A hope? How would you describe you deepest, most heartfelt 'wants' for yourself at the moment? For your family? For those who know you best? Are you happy (pleased) with what you *want*? Do you find your 'wants' consistent? Noble?

2. How would you prioritize your desire for 1) money, 2) wealth, 3) power? Is your *need* for each aligned with your desire (or craving, if appropriate) for each?

3. If money, wealth and power are not presently available to you in abundance, do you feel you would be equipped to handle them honorably if a windfall came your way? What makes you say so? What 'lens' or value system would drive your decision-making?

4. If you think Jeremiah 7 is stark, read Ezekiel 16!. Nowhere in the Bible does God more explicitly illustrate how brazen we are...and how desirous God is to redeem us.

5. Contention 10 raises many questions. What is your reaction now to the statement in Contention 1 that "morality is conditional"? Why do you think God may have made you that way?

6. "You want to pursue habits that are good for you, but there is only so much discipline to go around":

    - When are you best at controlling your self-interests? Under what conditions and environments?

- Consider and share: can you remember a time when you were overly focused on a situation in your life, and other areas suffered?

7. If you have a drive for leadership, where does it come from? What do you think is inside of you that desires this? What does it take to get your attention where matters of leadership are concerned? Are you happy with where you are looking for leadership in your life? Why or why not?

FURTHER READING:

For a brilliant and entertaining talk on discipline and moral authority, check out Frank Peretti's message titled *The Chair.* It's available in various video forms and as a download from Compass International.

Richard Rohr: *Falling Upward: A Spirituality for the Two Halves of Life* is an insightful book. I recommend it for a deeper read.

David Brooks: *The Road To Character,* 2015, Random House

Bob Buford: *Halftime: Moving From Success to Significance,* 2008, Zondervan

EPILOGUE

Scholars, doubters and common men have debated the contentions presented of BIMYTW for a long, long time. There is a mix of clever and meaningful quotes included in this project, but none more classic (or relevant, in my opinion) than the following passage from Epictetus. I include it here as an epilogue (due to its length) to help you appreciate just how *long* men have debated these subjects. While it is written in the 'classic' style of Epictetus' day, I encourage you to read through it with care. No author I've come across does a better job of summarizing the *exceptionality* of human thought and capability. In a mere four paragraphs, this crusty Greek stoic explains why man is *uniquely* privileged among all creation.

Of the things which are in our Power, and not in our Power, from **Discourses, Book One** (emphasis added, RDK)

Of all the faculties, you will find not one which is capable of contemplating itself; and, consequently, not capable either of approving or disapproving. How far does the grammatic art possess the contemplating power? As far as forming a judgement about what is written and spoken. And how for music? As far as judging about melody. Does either of them then contemplate itself? By no means. But **when you must write something to your friend, grammar will tell you what words you must write; but whether you should write or not, grammar will not tell you.** And so it is with music as to musical sounds; but whether you should sing at the present time and play on the lute, or do neither, music will not tell you. **What faculty then will tell you? That which contemplates both itself and all other things. And what is this faculty? The rational faculty; for this is the only faculty that we have received which examines itself, what it is, and what power it has, and what is the value of this gift, and examines all other faculties: for what else is there which tells us that golden things are beautiful, for they do not say so themselves? Evidently it is the faculty which is capable of judging of appearances. What else judges of music, grammar, and other faculties, proves their uses and points out the occasions for using them? Nothing else.**

As then it was fit to be so, that which is best of all and supreme over all is the only thing which the gods have placed in our power, the right use of appearances; but all other things they have not placed in our power. Was it because they did not choose? I indeed think that, if they had been able, they would have put these other things also in our power, but they certainly could not. For as we exist on the earth, and are bound to such a body and to such companions, how was it possible for us not to be hindered as to these things by externals?

But what says Zeus? "Epictetus, if it were possible, I would have made both your little body and your little property free and not exposed to hindrance. But now be not ignorant of this: this body is not yours, but it is clay finely tempered. And since I was not able to do for you what I have mentioned, **I have given you a small portion of us, this faculty of pursuing an object and avoiding it, and the faculty of desire and aversion, and, in a word, the faculty of using the appearances of things; and if you will take care of this faculty and consider it your only possession, you will never be hindered, never meet with impediments; you will not lament, you will not blame, you will not flatter any person.**

(Emphasis added)

References like that one help me appreciate that the stuff we ponder in our quiet moments are the *same things* that man has been pondering for ages. Whether or not Epictetus was the first to arrive at appreciating rational thought, what an incredible mind he must have had…back in A.D. 60-138.

You are surely evidence of Divine Creation! God Bless.

EPILOGUE 2

A quote from Frederick Buechner

It is a world of magic and mystery, of deep darkness and flickering starlight. It is a world where terrible things happen and wonderful things too. It is a world where goodness is pitted against evil, love against hate, order against chaos, in a great struggle where often it is hard to be sure who belongs to which side because appearances are endlessly deceptive. Yet for all its confusion and wildness, it is a world where the battle goes ultimately to the good, who live happily ever after, and where in the long run everybody, good and evil alike, becomes known by his true name . . . That is the fairy tale of the Gospel with, of course, one crucial difference from all other fairy tales, which is that the claim made for it is that it is true, that it not only happened once upon a time but has kept on happening ever since and is happening still.

- Frederick Buechner, *Telling the Truth*

ABOUT THE AUTHOR

R.D. 'Bob' Koncerak has led Christian study groups for more than thirty years. He has an MBA from Duquesne University and a bachelor's in Economics from Penn State. His first book, *The Most Fun I Never Want To Have Again*, was an *American Banker* Bestseller. Bob has been employed in the financial services industry for most of his so-called career. He is a proud father and grandfather who loves his family very much.

Printed in the United States
by Baker & Taylor Publisher Services